UPs & DOWNs

A JOURNAL FOR GOOD AND NOT-SO-GOOD DAYS

by Doro Ottermann

Chronicle Books
San Francisco

First published in the United States of America in 2017 by Chronicle Books LLC.

Original title: Tagebuch. Für gute und schlechte Tage by Doro Ottermann
© 2011 by Goldmann Verlag, a division of Verlagsgruppe Random House GmbH, München, Germany.

ISBN 978-1-4521-5466-4

MIX
Paper from
responsible sources

FSC™ C006948

Manufactured in China

Text and Illustrations by Doro Ottermann

10 9 8 7 6 5 4 3 2 1

Chronicle Books LLC
680 Second Street
San Francisco, CA 94107
www.chroniclebooks.com

This journal belongs to: ....

My goals and wishes: ....
....
....
....
....
....
....
....
....
....
....
....
....
....
....

This ruins my mood :

And this makes me happy:

This is the black cat
that crossed my path:

This went awry: ....
....
....

I couldn't help but laugh, despite it all, ☐ times.
About what? ....
....
....

I frittered away quite a bit of time doing this: ....
....
....

Do I regret it? ☐ yes ☐ no

This rubbed me the wrong way: ....
....
....

Three things I could do better tomorrow:
1. ....
2. ....
3. ....

I feel:

	yes	no	a bit
relaxed	☐	☐	☐
perplexed	☐	☐	☐
chatty	☐	☐	☐
charming	☐	☐	☐
exuberant	☐	☐	☐
outgoing	☐	☐	☐

	yes	no	a bit
feisty	☐	☐	☐
cheeky	☐	☐	☐
screwy	☐	☐	☐
brilliant	☐	☐	☐
motivated	☐	☐	☐
_____	☐	☐	☐

I met up with this many people: ☐ Names: ....
....

My favorite person to chat with: ....
I infected this many people with my good mood: ☐
Names: ....

What I did today to get closer to my goals: ....
....
....

Also, this happened: ....
....
....

I am excited for tomorrow, ☐ because ☐ even though ....
....

Date: _____   Time: _____

I feel:

	yes	no	a bit			yes	no	a bit
apathetic	☐	☐	☐	like a failure		☐	☐	☐
baffled	☐	☐	☐	resigned		☐	☐	☐
half-asleep	☐	☐	☐	hollow		☐	☐	☐
chaotic	☐	☐	☐	glum		☐	☐	☐
foolish	☐	☐	☐	inflexible		☐	☐	☐
lost	☐	☐	☐	_____		☐	☐	☐

I did this today: ....
....

And I would rather have done this: ....
....
....

I thought about whether I should ....
.... or not. Upon thorough reflection, I have
decided that ....
....

Do I have qualms about this? ☐ absolutely! ☐ minor ones
Why? ....
....

The lowest point of my day: ....
....
....

This is how far my leap of faith took me:

| 1 | 2 | 3 | 4 | 5 | 6 | 7 | 8 | 9 | 10 | 11 |

I am proud of myself for . . . .

. . . .

This was not ideal: . . . .

but this still worked out really well: . . . .

. . . .

. . . .

Something that motivated me: . . . .

. . . .

Three little things that brought me joy:

1. . . . .

2. . . . .

3. . . . .

I laughed ☐ times. About what? . . . .

. . . .

The highlight of my day: . . . .

. . . .

. . . .

I've had it up to here:
(Fill in level of fed-up-ness)

This wore me out today: ....
....
....

This was running through my mind at the time: ....
....
....

This went very wrong: ....
....

How difficult is it for me to think positively right now?
☐ extremely ☐ a little bit
Why? ....
....

Some space for general griping: ....
....
....

I feel:

	yes	no	a bit			yes	no	a bit
hopeful	☐	☐	☐	refreshed	☐	☐	☐
shy	☐	☐	☐	tame	☐	☐	☐
happy	☐	☐	☐	diligent	☐	☐	☐
focused	☐	☐	☐	generous	☐	☐	☐
respectable	☐	☐	☐	unique	☐	☐	☐
unforgettable	☐	☐	☐	_____	☐	☐	☐

I didn't let this stress me out at all: ....
....
....

Good news: ....
....
....

I'm flirting with the idea of ....
....
....
....

Here's how content I am: 0% [＿＿＿＿＿＿＿＿＿＿＿＿] 100%

Tomorrow will be a good day because ....
....
....

Date: _____   Time: _____

I feel:

	yes	no	a bit			yes	no	a bit
dreadful	☐	☐	☐		stingy	☐	☐	☐
uptight	☐	☐	☐		ugly	☐	☐	☐
naïve	☐	☐	☐		thin-skinned	☐	☐	☐
primitive	☐	☐	☐		spaced out	☐	☐	☐
bossy	☐	☐	☐		superfluous	☐	☐	☐
upset	☐	☐	☐		withdrawn	☐	☐	☐
even-keeled	☐	☐	☐		hormonal	☐	☐	☐
taciturn	☐	☐	☐		_____	☐	☐	☐

I would rather have done this differently: ....
....
....
....

Did I set the bar too high? ☐ yes ☐ no ☐ a bit
Details: ....
Am I plagued by doubts? ☐ yes ☐ no
Which ones? ....
It's really ☐ dramatic! ☐ not a big deal

Here's how stressed I am: 0% [   ] 100%

This is getting on my nerves: ....
....

Joy

happy as a clam ↑

down in the dumps

6 a.m.   9 a.m.   12 p.m.   3 p.m.   6 p.m.   9 p.m.   time of day

Things couldn't have gone better. This morning I ....

.... , afterward I

.... and in the evening I ....

....

This exceeded my expectations as well : ....

....

Could things have gone even better? ☐ yes ☐ no ☐ maybe
How? ....

....

Did anybody make me jump for joy? ☐ yes ☐ no
Who? With what? ....

....

Here's what I wish ☐ for tomorrow ☐ for the future : ....

....

....

Date : _____ Time : _____

Aches and pains :
(mark corresponding body parts)

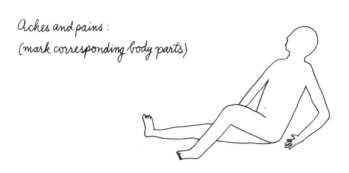

This is how much time I wasted

Working : __ hours   Brooding : __ hours
Eating : __ hours   Bickering : __ hours
Watching TV : __ hours   _____ : __ hours

Would I have preferred to stay in bed? ☐ yes ☐ no
Why? ....
....
My biggest fear right now is that ....
.... , but ....
....

I cried ☐ times. About what? ....
....

Biggest aggravation of the day : ....
....

I feel:

	yes	no	a bit
mellow	☐	☐	☐
peaceful	☐	☐	☐
caring	☐	☐	☐
attractive	☐	☐	☐
impressed	☐	☐	☐
honorable	☐	☐	☐
fancy	☐	☐	☐
adventurous	☐	☐	☐

	yes	no	a bit
quiet	☐	☐	☐
good	☐	☐	☐
sweet	☐	☐	☐
sassy	☐	☐	☐
productive	☐	☐	☐
phenomenal	☐	☐	☐
curious	☐	☐	☐
_____	☐	☐	☐

This made me pretty happy: ....
....

And this made me laugh: ....
....

Did I surprise myself? ☐ yes ☐ no
How so? ....

I deserve a medal for: ....
....

Tomorrow I might: ....
....
....

Date: _____ Time: _____

I feel:

	yes	no	a bit			yes	no	a bit
slow	☐	☐	☐		sensitive	☐	☐	☐
stubborn	☐	☐	☐		disappointed	☐	☐	☐
lonely	☐	☐	☐		fussy	☐	☐	☐
phony	☐	☐	☐		furious	☐	☐	☐
moronic	☐	☐	☐		naughty	☐	☐	☐
sharp	☐	☐	☐		haughty	☐	☐	☐
listless	☐	☐	☐		misanthropic	☐	☐	☐
antagonistic	☐	☐	☐		_____	☐	☐	☐

I felt down on my luck when: ....
....

And here's what was lacking: ....
....

I am generally ☐ unsatisfied ☐ satisfied with life because: ....
....
....

Do I wish I could be someone else? ☐ yes ☐ no
If yes, whom? ....

Am I annoyed by someone else's good mood? ☐ yes ☐ no
If yes, why? ....

This is how happy I feel:
(draw your expression)

If my mood were a color, it would be: ....

Did someone compliment me? ☐ yes ☐ no
If yes, on what? ....
And now it's time to pay myself a compliment or two!
One thing I did well: ....
....)

and kudos to me for ....
....

Small mishap: ....
....)
but here's the upside: ....
....

The three best things that happened today:
1 ....
2 ....
3 ....

Date: _____   Time: _____

Mood:

sort of OK ↑

really lousy _____→ time of day
            6 a.m. 9 a.m. 12 p.m. 3 p.m. 6 p.m. 9 p.m.

I didn't like this at all: ....
....
.... Oh well!

I told .... exactly what I think about
....

Now I feel ☐ better ☐ worse ☐ the same as before

Unfortunately, I wasn't able to ....
....
...., but tomorrow I'll probably manage it.

This gave me food for thought: ....
....

Suggested improvements for ☐ tomorrow ☐ the future: ....
....
....

I feel:

	yes	no	a bit		yes	no	a bit
joyful	☐	☐	☐	funny	☐	☐	☐
creative	☐	☐	☐	free	☐	☐	☐
ambitious	☐	☐	☐	dazzling	☐	☐	☐
ordinary	☐	☐	☐	clever	☐	☐	☐
alert	☐	☐	☐	efficient	☐	☐	☐
exotic	☐	☐	☐	cautious	☐	☐	☐
satisfied	☐	☐	☐	sophisticated	☐	☐	☐
mysterious	☐	☐	☐	_____	☐	☐	☐

Have I outdone myself? ☐ yes ☐ no

If yes, how? ....

....

The nicest thought of the day: ....

....

Three things that made me happy:

1. ....

2. ....

3. ....

I'm looking forward to: ....

....

Date: _____   Time: _____

I feel:

	yes	no	a bit
bad	☐	☐	☐
prickly	☐	☐	☐
resigned	☐	☐	☐
unsatisfied	☐	☐	☐
decadent	☐	☐	☐
pensive	☐	☐	☐

	yes	no	a bit
gloomy	☐	☐	☐
empty	☐	☐	☐
indignant	☐	☐	☐
secretive	☐	☐	☐
mild	☐	☐	☐
_____	☐	☐	☐

This rained on my parade: ....
....

I view this as ☐ a problem ☐ a challenge, because ....
....

The future looks
☐ bleak ☐ bright ☐ filled with shimmering shades of gray

Would I rather be elsewhere right now? ☐ yes ☐ no
If yes, where and why? ....
....

The most annoying person I talked to: ....

The biggest disappointment of the day: ....
....

This is me riding the wave of success :

This was quite good : ....
....
This unfortunately less so : ....
...., but it doesn't matter.

Did I reward myself ? ☐ yes ☐ no
If yes, how and for what ? ....
....
If no, why not ? ....
....

Here's how relaxed I feel : 0% [   ] 100%

I enjoyed this : ....
....

My resolution for tomorrow : ....
....

This is how much I have on my plate right now :

This put me in a really bad mood : ....
....

Especially because : ....
I would categorize the situation as a ☐ mountain ☐ molehill

I saw these people : ....
....

But I would rather have seen these people : ....
....

Three things that got on my nerves :
1. ....
2. ....
3. ....

I am this frustrated : 0% [   ] 100%

This is what I'm dreading (somewhat): ....
....

I feel:

	yes	no	a bit		yes	no	a bit
big-hearted	☐	☐	☐	patient	☐	☐	☐
gullible	☐	☐	☐	friendly	☐	☐	☐
reckless	☐	☐	☐	beloved	☐	☐	☐
cheerful	☐	☐	☐	strong	☐	☐	☐
trivial	☐	☐	☐	ethereal	☐	☐	☐
cautious	☐	☐	☐	————	☐	☐	☐

Have I come closer to reaching my goals? ☐ yes ☐ no

How so? ....

Did I get distracted? ☐ of course not ☐ maybe a little

By what? ....

....

This couldn't have gone better: ....

....

Three things I am very satisfied with:

1. ....

2. ....

3. ....

This day was ☐ good ☐ crazy good because ....

....

....

Date : _____   Time : _____

I feel :

	yes	no	a bit			yes	no	a bit
dishonest	☐	☐	☐	restless		☐	☐	☐
static	☐	☐	☐	skeptical		☐	☐	☐
beat	☐	☐	☐	sentimental		☐	☐	☐
bored	☐	☐	☐	intelligent		☐	☐	☐
ornery	☐	☐	☐	flabbergasted		☐	☐	☐
contrite	☐	☐	☐	_____		☐	☐	☐

From the moment I woke up, I was annoyed by ....
.... Around noon,
I unfortunately ....
and in the evening I was just glad that ....
....

Anything else? ....
....
....

How well did I fail today?
☐ horribly   ☐ passably   ☐ brilliantly   ☐ _____

What am I afraid of and why? ....
....
....

I had this many bright ideas today:
(draw a lightbulb for each idea)

Here's what I spent my time doing:
Eating: __ hours   Being happy: __ hours
Sleeping: __ hours   Being lazy: __ hours
Reading: __ hours   _____: __ hours

Today, not only did I ....
....
but I also ....
....
I'm ☐ very ☐ a little bit proud of myself for it.

☐ % go-getter + ☐ % couch potato = 100% me!

This made me laugh: ....
....

This day was my friend because ....
....
....

Date: _____   Time: _____

This is the black cat
that crossed my path:

This went awry: ....
....
....

I couldn't help but laugh, despite it all, ☐ times.
About what? ....
....
....

I frittered away quite a bit of time doing this: ....
....
....

Do I regret it? ☐ yes ☐ no

This rubbed me the wrong way: ....
....
....

Three things I could do better tomorrow:
1. ....
2. ....
3. ....

I feel:

	yes	no	a bit			yes	no	a bit
relaxed	☐	☐	☐	feisty		☐	☐	☐
perplexed	☐	☐	☐	cheeky		☐	☐	☐
chatty	☐	☐	☐	screwy		☐	☐	☐
charming	☐	☐	☐	brilliant		☐	☐	☐
exuberant	☐	☐	☐	motivated		☐	☐	☐
outgoing	☐	☐	☐	————		☐	☐	☐

I met up with this many people: ☐ Names: ....
....

My favorite person to chat with: ....
I infected this many people with my good mood: ☐
Names: ....

What I did today to get closer to my goals: ....
....
....
....

Also, this happened: ....
....
....

I am excited for tomorrow, ☐ because ☐ even though ....
....

Date: _____ Time: _____

I feel:

	yes	no	a bit			yes	no	a bit
apathetic	☐	☐	☐	like a failure	☐	☐	☐
baffled	☐	☐	☐	resigned	☐	☐	☐
half-asleep	☐	☐	☐	hollow	☐	☐	☐
chaotic	☐	☐	☐	glum	☐	☐	☐
foolish	☐	☐	☐	inflexible	☐	☐	☐
lost	☐	☐	☐	_____	☐	☐	☐

I did this today: ....
....

And I would rather have done this: ....
....

I thought about whether I should ....
.... or not. Upon thorough reflection, I have
decided that ....
....

Do I have qualms about this? ☐ absolutely! ☐ minor ones
Why? ....
....

The lowest point of my day: ....
....
....

This is how far my leap of faith took me:

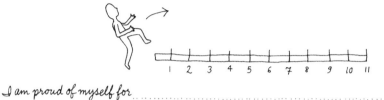

1 2 3 4 5 6 7 8 9 10 11

I am proud of myself for ....
....

This was not ideal: ....

but this still worked out really well: ....
....
....

Something that motivated me: ....
....

Three little things that brought me joy:

1. ....
2. ....
3. ....

I laughed ☐ times. About what? ....
....

The highlight of my day: ....
....
....

Date : _____ Time : _____

I've had it up to here :
(Fill in level of fed-up-ness)

This wore me out today : ....
....
....

This was running through my mind at the time : ....
....
....
....

This went very wrong : ....
....
....

How difficult is it for me to think positively right now ?
☐ extremely ☐ a little bit
Why? ....
....

Some space for general griping : ....
....
....

I feel:

	yes	no	a bit			yes	no	a bit
hopeful	☐	☐	☐	refreshed	☐	☐	☐
shy	☐	☐	☐	tame	☐	☐	☐
happy	☐	☐	☐	diligent	☐	☐	☐
focused	☐	☐	☐	generous	☐	☐	☐
respectable	☐	☐	☐	unique	☐	☐	☐
unforgettable	☐	☐	☐	_____	☐	☐	☐

I didn't let this stress me out at all: ....
....
....

Good news: ....
....
....

I'm flirting with the idea of ....
....
....
....

Here's how content I am: 0% [   ] 100%

Tomorrow will be a good day because ....
....
....

Date: _____   Time: _____

I feel:

	yes	no	a bit		yes	no	a bit
dreadful	☐	☐	☐	stingy	☐	☐	☐
uptight	☐	☐	☐	ugly	☐	☐	☐
naïve	☐	☐	☐	thin-skinned	☐	☐	☐
primitive	☐	☐	☐	spaced out	☐	☐	☐
bossy	☐	☐	☐	superfluous	☐	☐	☐
upset	☐	☐	☐	withdrawn	☐	☐	☐
even-keeled	☐	☐	☐	hormonal	☐	☐	☐
taciturn	☐	☐	☐	_____	☐	☐	☐

I would rather have done this differently: ....
....
....
....

Did I set the bar too high? ☐ yes ☐ no ☐ a bit
Details: ....
Am I plagued by doubts? ☐ yes ☐ no
Which ones? ....
It's really ☐ dramatic! ☐ not a big deal

Here's how stressed I am: 0% [_____] 100%

This is getting on my nerves: ....
....

Joy

happy
as a clam

down in
the dumps

6 a.m.　9 a.m.　12 p.m.　3 p.m.　6 p.m.　9 p.m.　time of
day

Things couldn't have gone better. This morning I ....
...., afterward I
.... and in the evening I ....
....

This exceeded my expectations as well: ....
....

Could things have gone even better? ☐ yes ☐ no ☐ maybe
How? ....
....

Did anybody make me jump for joy? ☐ yes ☐ no
Who? With what? ....
....

Here's what I wish ☐ for tomorrow ☐ for the future: ....
....
....

Aches and pains :
(mark corresponding body parts)

This is how much time I wasted

Working: __ hours   Brooding: __ hours

Eating: __ hours   Bickering: __ hours

Watching TV: __ hours   _____: __ hours

Would I have preferred to stay in bed? ☐ yes ☐ no

Why? ....

....

My biggest fear right now is that ....

...., but ....

....

I cried ☐ times. About what? ....

....

Biggest aggravation of the day: ....

....

I feel:

	yes	no	a bit			yes	no	a bit
mellow	☐	☐	☐	quiet	☐	☐	☐
peaceful	☐	☐	☐	good	☐	☐	☐
caring	☐	☐	☐	sweet	☐	☐	☐
attractive	☐	☐	☐	sassy	☐	☐	☐
impressed	☐	☐	☐	productive	☐	☐	☐
honorable	☐	☐	☐	phenomenal	☐	☐	☐
fancy	☐	☐	☐	curious	☐	☐	☐
adventurous	☐	☐	☐	_____	☐	☐	☐

This made me pretty happy: ....

....

And this made me laugh: ....

....

Did I surprise myself? ☐ yes ☐ no

How so? ....

I deserve a medal for: ....

....

Tomorrow I might: ....

....

....

Date: _____   Time: _____

I feel:

	yes	no	a bit			yes	no	a bit
slow	☐	☐	☐		sensitive	☐	☐	☐
stubborn	☐	☐	☐		disappointed	☐	☐	☐
lonely	☐	☐	☐		fussy	☐	☐	☐
phony	☐	☐	☐		furious	☐	☐	☐
moronic	☐	☐	☐		naughty	☐	☐	☐
sharp	☐	☐	☐		haughty	☐	☐	☐
listless	☐	☐	☐		misanthropic	☐	☐	☐
antagonistic	☐	☐	☐		_____	☐	☐	☐

I felt down on my luck when: ....
....

And here's what was lacking: ....
....

I am generally ☐ unsatisfied ☐ satisfied with life because: ....
....
....

Do I wish I could be someone else? ☐ yes ☐ no
If yes, whom? ....

Am I annoyed by someone else's good mood? ☐ yes ☐ no
If yes, why? ....

This is how happy I feel:
(draw your expression)

If my mood were a color, it would be: ....

Did someone compliment me? ☐ yes ☐ no
If yes, on what? ....
And now it's time to pay myself a compliment or two!
One thing I did well: ....

....)

and kudos to me for ....

....

Small mishap: ....

....)

but here's the upside: ....

....

The three best things that happened today:
1 ....
2 ....
3 ....

Date: _____ Time: _____

Mood:

sort of OK ↑

really lousy ⊢————————————————————→ time of
             6 a.m. 9 a.m. 12 p.m. 3 p.m. 6 p.m. 9 p.m.   day

I didn't like this at all : ....
....
.... Oh well!

I told .... exactly what I think about
....

Now I feel ☐ better ☐ worse ☐ the same as before

Unfortunately, I wasn't able to ....
....
...., but tomorrow I'll probably manage it.

This gave me food for thought : ....
....

Suggested improvements for ☐ tomorrow ☐ the future : ....
....
....

I feel:

	yes	no	a bit			yes	no	a bit
joyful	☐	☐	☐	funny		☐	☐	☐
creative	☐	☐	☐	free		☐	☐	☐
ambitious	☐	☐	☐	dazzling		☐	☐	☐
ordinary	☐	☐	☐	clever		☐	☐	☐
alert	☐	☐	☐	efficient		☐	☐	☐
exotic	☐	☐	☐	cautious		☐	☐	☐
satisfied	☐	☐	☐	sophisticated		☐	☐	☐
mysterious	☐	☐	☐	_____		☐	☐	☐

Have I outdone myself? ☐ yes ☐ no

If yes, how? ....
....

The nicest thought of the day: ....
....

Three things that made me happy:

1. ....
2. ....
3. ....

I'm looking forward to: ....
....

Date: _____ Time: _____

I feel:

	yes	no	a bit			yes	no	a bit
bad	☐	☐	☐	gloomy		☐	☐	☐
prickly	☐	☐	☐	empty		☐	☐	☐
resigned	☐	☐	☐	indignant		☐	☐	☐
unsatisfied	☐	☐	☐	secretive		☐	☐	☐
decadent	☐	☐	☐	mild		☐	☐	☐
pensive	☐	☐	☐	_____		☐	☐	☐

This rained on my parade: ....
....

I view this as ☐ a problem ☐ a challenge, because ....
....

The future looks
☐ bleak ☐ bright ☐ filled with shimmering shades of gray

Would I rather be elsewhere right now? ☐ yes ☐ no
If yes, where and why? ....
....

The most annoying person I talked to: ....

The biggest disappointment of the day: ....
....

This is me riding the wave of success:

This was quite good: ....
....

This unfortunately less so: ....
...., but it doesn't matter.

Did I reward myself? ☐ yes ☐ no
If yes, how and for what? ....
....

If no, why not? ....
....

Here's how relaxed I feel: 0% [   ] 100%

I enjoyed this: ....
....

My resolution for tomorrow: ....
....

Date : _____ Time : _____

This is how much I have on my plate right now :

This put me in a really bad mood : ....
....

Especially because : ....
I would categorize the situation as a ☐ mountain ☐ molehill

I saw these people : ....
....

But I would rather have seen these people : ....
....

Three things that got on my nerves :

1. ....
2. ....
3. ....

I am this frustrated : 0% [   ] 100%

This is what I'm dreading (somewhat) : ....
....

I feel:

	yes	no	a bit			yes	no	a bit
big-hearted	☐	☐	☐		patient	☐	☐	☐
gullible	☐	☐	☐		friendly	☐	☐	☐
reckless	☐	☐	☐		beloved	☐	☐	☐
cheerful	☐	☐	☐		strong	☐	☐	☐
trivial	☐	☐	☐		ethereal	☐	☐	☐
cautious	☐	☐	☐		————	☐	☐	☐

Have I come closer to reaching my goals? ☐ yes ☐ no

How so? . . . .

Did I get distracted? ☐ of course not ☐ maybe a little

By what? . . . .

. . . .

This couldn't have gone better: . . . .

. . . .

Three things I am very satisfied with:

1. . . . .

2. . . . .

3. . . . .

This day was ☐ good ☐ crazy good because . . . .

. . . .

. . . .

Date: _____ Time: _____

I feel:

	yes	no	a bit			yes	no	a bit
dishonest	☐	☐	☐	restless		☐	☐	☐
static	☐	☐	☐	skeptical		☐	☐	☐
beat	☐	☐	☐	sentimental		☐	☐	☐
bored	☐	☐	☐	intelligent		☐	☐	☐
ornery	☐	☐	☐	flabbergasted		☐	☐	☐
contrite	☐	☐	☐	_____		☐	☐	☐

From the moment I woke up, I was annoyed by ....
.... Around noon,
I unfortunately ....
and in the evening I was just glad that ....
....

Anything else? ....
....
....

How well did I fail today?
☐ horribly   ☐ passably   ☐ brilliantly   ☐ _____

What am I afraid of and why? ....
....
....

I had this many bright ideas today:
(draw a lightbulb for each idea)

Here's what I spent my time doing:
Eating: __ hours   Being happy: __ hours
Sleeping: __ hours   Being lazy: __ hours
Reading: __ hours   _____: __ hours

Today, not only did I ....

but I also ....

I'm ☐ very ☐ a little bit proud of myself for it.

☐ % go-getter + ☐ % couch potato = 100% me!

This made me laugh: ....

....

This day was my friend because ....

....

....

A sampling of my bad moods :

When ?...

Reason :..

....

When ?...

Reason :..

....

When?...

Reason :..

....

When ?...

Reason :..

....

When?...

Reason :..

....

When ?...

Reason :..

....

A sampling of my good moods:

When? . . . .

Reason : . . . .

. . . .

When? . . . .

Reason : . . . .

. . . .

When? . . . .

Reason : . . . .

. . . .

When? . . . .

Reason : . . . .

. . . .

When? . . . .

Reason : . . . .

. . . .

When? . . . .

Reason : . . . .

. . . .

<u>Date :</u>   Time :

This is the black cat
that crossed my path :

This went awry : ....
....
....

I couldn't help but laugh, despite it all, ☐ times.
About what? ....
....
....

I frittered away quite a bit of time doing this : ....
....
....

Do I regret it? ☐ yes ☐ no

This rubbed me the wrong way : ....
....
....

Three things I could do better tomorrow :
1. ....
2. ....
3. ....

→ I feel:

	yes	no	a bit			yes	no	a bit
relaxed	☐	☐	☐	feisty		☐	☐	☐
perplexed	☐	☐	☐	cheeky		☐	☐	☐
chatty	☐	☐	☐	screwy		☐	☐	☐
charming	☐	☐	☐	brilliant		☐	☐	☐
exuberant	☐	☐	☐	motivated		☐	☐	☐
outgoing	☐	☐	☐	———		☐	☐	☐

I met up with this many people: ☐ Names: ....
....

My favorite person to chat with: ....
I infected this many people with my good mood: ☐
Names: ....

What I did today to get closer to my goals: ....
....
....

Also, this happened: ....
....
....

I am excited for tomorrow, ☐ because ☐ even though ....
....

Date: _____   Time: _____

I feel:

	yes	no	a bit			yes	no	a bit
apathetic	☐	☐	☐	like a failure		☐	☐	☐
baffled	☐	☐	☐	resigned		☐	☐	☐
half-asleep	☐	☐	☐	hollow		☐	☐	☐
chaotic	☐	☐	☐	glum		☐	☐	☐
foolish	☐	☐	☐	inflexible		☐	☐	☐
lost	☐	☐	☐	_____		☐	☐	☐

I did this today: ....
....

And I would rather have done this: ....
....
....

I thought about whether I should ....
.... or not. Upon thorough reflection, I have

decided that ....
....

Do I have qualms about this? ☐ absolutely! ☐ minor ones

Why? ....
....

The lowest point of my day: ....
....
....

This is how far my leap of faith took me:

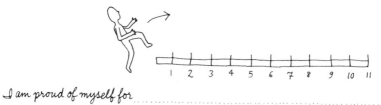

1 2 3 4 5 6 7 8 9 10 11

I am proud of myself for ....

....

This was not ideal: ....

but this still worked out really well: ....

....

....

Something that motivated me: ....

....

Three little things that brought me joy:

1. ....

2. ....

3. ....

I laughed ☐ times. About what? ....

....

The highlight of my day: ....

....

....

<u>Date:</u>   Time:

I've had it up to here:
(Fill in level of fed-up-ness)

This wore me out today: ....
....
....

This was running through my mind at the time: ....
....
....
....

This went very wrong: ....
....
....

How difficult is it for me to think positively right now?
☐ extremely ☐ a little bit
Why? ....
....

Some space for general griping: ....
....
....

I feel:

	yes	no	a bit			yes	no	a bit
hopeful	☐	☐	☐	refreshed	☐	☐	☐
shy	☐	☐	☐	tame	☐	☐	☐
happy	☐	☐	☐	diligent	☐	☐	☐
focused	☐	☐	☐	generous	☐	☐	☐
respectable	☐	☐	☐	unique	☐	☐	☐
unforgettable	☐	☐	☐	_____	☐	☐	☐

I didn't let this stress me out at all: ....

....

....

Good news: ....

....

....

I'm flirting with the idea of ....

....

....

....

Here's how content I am: 0% [_____] 100%

Tomorrow will be a good day because ....

....

....

Date: _____   Time: _____

I feel:

	yes	no	a bit			yes	no	a bit
dreadful	☐	☐	☐	stingy		☐	☐	☐
uptight	☐	☐	☐	ugly		☐	☐	☐
naïve	☐	☐	☐	thin-skinned		☐	☐	☐
primitive	☐	☐	☐	spaced out		☐	☐	☐
bossy	☐	☐	☐	superfluous		☐	☐	☐
upset	☐	☐	☐	withdrawn		☐	☐	☐
even-keeled	☐	☐	☐	hormonal		☐	☐	☐
taciturn	☐	☐	☐	_____		☐	☐	☐

I would rather have done this differently: ....
....
....
....

Did I set the bar too high? ☐ yes ☐ no ☐ a bit
Details: ....
Am I plagued by doubts? ☐ yes ☐ no
Which ones? ....
It's really ☐ dramatic! ☐ not a big deal

Here's how stressed I am: 0% [   ] 100%

This is getting on my nerves: ....
....

Joy

happy
as a clam ↑

down in
the dumps

6 a.m.   9 a.m.   12 p.m.   3 p.m.   6 p.m.   9 p.m.   time of
day

Things couldn't have gone better. This morning I ....
...., afterward I
.... and in the evening I ....
....

This exceeded my expectations as well: ....
....

Could things have gone even better? ☐ yes ☐ no ☐ maybe
How? ....
....

Did anybody make me jump for joy? ☐ yes ☐ no
Who? With what? ....
....

Here's what I wish ☐ for tomorrow ☐ for the future: ....
....
....

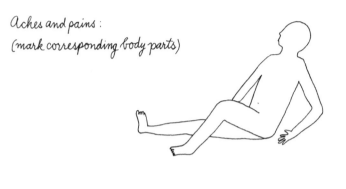

Date: _____   Time: _____

Aches and pains:
(mark corresponding body parts)

This is how much time I wasted

Working: __ hours   Brooding: __ hours
Eating: __ hours   Bickering: __ hours
Watching TV: __ hours   _____: __ hours

Would I have preferred to stay in bed? ☐ yes ☐ no
Why? ....
....
My biggest fear right now is that ....
.... , but ....
....

I cried ☐ times. About what? ....
....

Biggest aggravation of the day: ....
....

I feel:

	yes	no	a bit			yes	no	a bit
mellow	☐	☐	☐	quiet	☐	☐	☐
peaceful	☐	☐	☐	good	☐	☐	☐
caring	☐	☐	☐	sweet	☐	☐	☐
attractive	☐	☐	☐	sassy	☐	☐	☐
impressed	☐	☐	☐	productive	☐	☐	☐
honorable	☐	☐	☐	phenomenal	☐	☐	☐
fancy	☐	☐	☐	curious	☐	☐	☐
adventurous	☐	☐	☐	_____	☐	☐	☐

This made me pretty happy: ....
....

And this made me laugh: ....
....

Did I surprise myself? ☐ yes ☐ no
How so? ....

I deserve a medal for: ....
....

Tomorrow I might: ....
....
....

Date: _____   Time: _____

I feel:

	yes	no	a bit			yes	no	a bit
slow	☐	☐	☐	sensitive	☐	☐	☐
stubborn	☐	☐	☐	disappointed	☐	☐	☐
lonely	☐	☐	☐	fussy	☐	☐	☐
phony	☐	☐	☐	furious	☐	☐	☐
moronic	☐	☐	☐	naughty	☐	☐	☐
sharp	☐	☐	☐	haughty	☐	☐	☐
listless	☐	☐	☐	misanthropic	☐	☐	☐
antagonistic	☐	☐	☐	_____	☐	☐	☐

I felt down on my luck when: ....
....

And here's what was lacking: ....
....

I am generally ☐ unsatisfied ☐ satisfied with life because: ....
....
....

Do I wish I could be someone else? ☐ yes ☐ no
If yes, whom? ....

Am I annoyed by someone else's good mood? ☐ yes ☐ no
If yes, why? ....

This is how happy I feel:
(draw your expression)

If my mood were a color, it would be: ....

Did someone compliment me? ☐ yes ☐ no
If yes, on what? ....
And now it's time to pay myself a compliment or two!
One thing I did well: ....

....)

and kudos to me for ....

....

Small mishap: ....

....,

but here's the upside: ....

....

The three best things that happened today:
1. ....
2. ....
3. ....

Date: _____   Time: _____

Mood:

sort of OK ↑

really lousy
  |————|————|————|————|————|————|————→ time of
     6 a.m. 9 a.m. 12 p.m. 3 p.m. 6 p.m. 9 p.m.   day

I didn't like this at all: ....
....
.... Oh well!

I told .... exactly what I think about
....

Now I feel ☐ better ☐ worse ☐ the same as before

Unfortunately, I wasn't able to ....
....
.................................., but tomorrow I'll probably manage it.

This gave me food for thought: ....
....

Suggested improvements for ☐ tomorrow ☐ the future: ....
....
....

I feel:

	yes	no	a bit
joyful	☐	☐	☐
creative	☐	☐	☐
ambitious	☐	☐	☐
ordinary	☐	☐	☐
alert	☐	☐	☐
exotic	☐	☐	☐
satisfied	☐	☐	☐
mysterious	☐	☐	☐

	yes	no	a bit
funny	☐	☐	☐
free	☐	☐	☐
dazzling	☐	☐	☐
clever	☐	☐	☐
efficient	☐	☐	☐
cautious	☐	☐	☐
sophisticated	☐	☐	☐
————	☐	☐	☐

Have I outdone myself? ☐ yes ☐ no

If yes, how? ....

....

The nicest thought of the day: ....

....

Three things that made me happy:

1. ....

2. ....

3. ....

I'm looking forward to: ....

....

Date: _____   Time: _____

I feel:

	yes	no	a bit
bad	☐	☐	☐
prickly	☐	☐	☐
resigned	☐	☐	☐
unsatisfied	☐	☐	☐
decadent	☐	☐	☐
pensive	☐	☐	☐

	yes	no	a bit
gloomy	☐	☐	☐
empty	☐	☐	☐
indignant	☐	☐	☐
secretive	☐	☐	☐
mild	☐	☐	☐
_____	☐	☐	☐

This rained on my parade: ....
....

I view this as ☐ a problem ☐ a challenge, because ....
....

The future looks
☐ bleak ☐ bright ☐ filled with shimmering shades of gray

Would I rather be elsewhere right now? ☐ yes ☐ no
If yes, where and why? ....
....

The most annoying person I talked to: ....

The biggest disappointment of the day: ....
....

This is me riding the wave of success :

This was quite good : ....
....
This unfortunately less so : ....
...., but it doesn't matter.

Did I reward myself ? ☐ yes ☐ no
If yes, how and for what ? ....
....
If no, why not ? ....
....

Here's how relaxed I feel : 0% [   ] 100%

I enjoyed this : ....
....

My resolution for tomorrow : ....
....

Date: _____   Time: _____

This is how much I have on my plate right now:

This put me in a really bad mood: ....
....

Especially because: ....
I would categorize the situation as a ☐ mountain ☐ molehill

I saw these people: ....
....

But I would rather have seen these people: ....
....

Three things that got on my nerves:
1. ....
2. ....
3. ....

I am this frustrated: 0% [   ] 100%

This is what I'm dreading (somewhat): ....
....

I feel:

	yes	no	a bit			yes	no	a bit
big-hearted	☐	☐	☐	patient	☐	☐	☐
gullible	☐	☐	☐	friendly	☐	☐	☐
reckless	☐	☐	☐	beloved	☐	☐	☐
cheerful	☐	☐	☐	strong	☐	☐	☐
trivial	☐	☐	☐	ethereal	☐	☐	☐
cautious	☐	☐	☐	————	☐	☐	☐

Have I come closer to reaching my goals? ☐ yes ☐ no

How so? ....

Did I get distracted? ☐ of course not ☐ maybe a little

By what? ....

....

This couldn't have gone better: ....

....

Three things I am very satisfied with:

1. ....
2. ....
3. ....

This day was ☐ good ☐ crazy good because ....

....

....

Date: _____   Time: _____

I feel:

	yes	no	a bit		yes	no	a bit
dishonest	☐	☐	☐	restless	☐	☐	☐
static	☐	☐	☐	skeptical	☐	☐	☐
beat	☐	☐	☐	sentimental	☐	☐	☐
bored	☐	☐	☐	intelligent	☐	☐	☐
ornery	☐	☐	☐	flabbergasted	☐	☐	☐
contrite	☐	☐	☐	_____	☐	☐	☐

From the moment I woke up, I was annoyed by ....
.... Around noon,
I unfortunately ....
and in the evening I was just glad that ....
....

Anything else? ....
....
....

How well did I fail today?
☐ horribly ☐ passably ☐ brilliantly ☐ _____

What am I afraid of and why? ....
....
....

I had this many bright ideas today:
(draw a lightbulb for each idea)

Here's what I spent my time doing:

Eating: ___ hours   Being happy: ___ hours
Sleeping: ___ hours   Being lazy: ___ hours
Reading: ___ hours   _____ : ___ hours

Today, not only did I ....

....

but I also ....

....

I'm ☐ very ☐ a little bit proud of myself for it.

☐ % go-getter + ☐ % couch potato = 100% me!

This made me laugh: ....

....

This day was my friend because ....

....

....

This is the black cat
that crossed my path:

This went awry: ....
....
....

I couldn't help but laugh, despite it all, ☐ times.
About what? ....
....
....

I frittered away quite a bit of time doing this: ....
....
....

Do I regret it? ☐ yes ☐ no

This rubbed me the wrong way: ....
....
....

Three things I could do better tomorrow:
1. ....
2. ....
3. ....

I feel:

	yes	no	a bit			yes	no	a bit
relaxed	☐	☐	☐	feisty		☐	☐	☐
perplexed	☐	☐	☐	cheeky		☐	☐	☐
chatty	☐	☐	☐	screwy		☐	☐	☐
charming	☐	☐	☐	brilliant		☐	☐	☐
exuberant	☐	☐	☐	motivated		☐	☐	☐
outgoing	☐	☐	☐	_____		☐	☐	☐

I met up with this many people: ☐ Names: ....
....

My favorite person to chat with: ....
I infected this many people with my good mood: ☐
Names: ....

What I did today to get closer to my goals: ....
....
....

Also, this happened: ....
....
....

I am excited for tomorrow, ☐ because ☐ even though ....
....

I feel:

	yes	no	a bit		yes	no	a bit
apathetic	☐	☐	☐	like a failure	☐	☐	☐
baffled	☐	☐	☐	resigned	☐	☐	☐
half-asleep	☐	☐	☐	hollow	☐	☐	☐
chaotic	☐	☐	☐	glum	☐	☐	☐
foolish	☐	☐	☐	inflexible	☐	☐	☐
lost	☐	☐	☐	_____	☐	☐	☐

I did this today: ....

....

And I would rather have done this: ....

....

....

I thought about whether I should ....

.... or not. Upon thorough reflection, I have

decided that ....

....

Do I have qualms about this? ☐ absolutely! ☐ minor ones

Why? ....

....

The lowest point of my day: ....

....

....

This is how far my leap of faith took me:

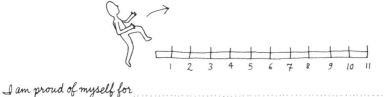

1 2 3 4 5 6 7 8 9 10 11

I am proud of myself for ....
....

This was not ideal: ....
but this still worked out really well: ....
....
....

Something that motivated me: ....
....

Three little things that brought me joy:

1. ....
2. ....
3. ....

I laughed ☐ times. About what? ....
....

The highlight of my day: ....
....
....

Date: _____ Time: _____

I've had it up to here:
(Fill in level of fed-up-ness)

This wore me out today: ....

....

....

This was running through my mind at the time: ....

....

....

....

This went very wrong: ....

....

....

How difficult is it for me to think positively right now?
☐ extremely ☐ a little bit
Why? ....

....

Some space for general griping: ....

....

....

I feel:

	yes	no	a bit			yes	no	a bit
hopeful	☐	☐	☐	refreshed	☐	☐	☐
shy	☐	☐	☐	tame	☐	☐	☐
happy	☐	☐	☐	diligent	☐	☐	☐
focused	☐	☐	☐	generous	☐	☐	☐
respectable	☐	☐	☐	unique	☐	☐	☐
unforgettable	☐	☐	☐	_____	☐	☐	☐

I didn't let this stress me out at all: ....
....
....

Good news: ....
....
....

I'm flirting with the idea of ....
....
....
....

Here's how content I am: 0% [_____] 100%

Tomorrow will be a good day because ....
....
....

Date: _____   Time: _____

I feel:

	yes	no	a bit			yes	no	a bit
dreadful	☐	☐	☐		stingy	☐	☐	☐
uptight	☐	☐	☐		ugly	☐	☐	☐
naïve	☐	☐	☐		thin-skinned	☐	☐	☐
primitive	☐	☐	☐		spaced out	☐	☐	☐
bossy	☐	☐	☐		superfluous	☐	☐	☐
upset	☐	☐	☐		withdrawn	☐	☐	☐
even-keeled	☐	☐	☐		hormonal	☐	☐	☐
taciturn	☐	☐	☐		_____	☐	☐	☐

I would rather have done this differently: ....

....

....

....

Did I set the bar too high? ☐ yes ☐ no ☐ a bit

Details: ....

Am I plagued by doubts? ☐ yes ☐ no

Which ones? ....

It's really ☐ dramatic! ☐ not a big deal

Here's how stressed I am: 0% [_____] 100%

This is getting on my nerves: ....

....

Joy

happy
as a clam

down in
the dumps

6 a.m.   9 a.m.   12 p.m.   3 p.m.   6 p.m.   9 p.m.   time of
                                                      day

Things couldn't have gone better. This morning I ....
...., afterward I
.... and in the evening I ....
....

This exceeded my expectations as well: ....
....

Could things have gone even better? ☐ yes ☐ no ☐ maybe
How? ....
....

Did anybody make me jump for joy? ☐ yes ☐ no
Who? With what? ....
....

Here's what I wish ☐ for tomorrow ☐ for the future: ....
....
....

Date: _____ Time: _____

Aches and pains :
(mark corresponding body parts)

This is how much time I wasted

Working: __ hours   Brooding: __hours
Eating: __hours   Bickering: __hours
Watching TV: __hours   _____: __hours

Would I have preferred to stay in bed? ☐ yes ☐ no
Why? ....
....

My biggest fear right now is that ....
...., but ....
....

I cried ☐ times. About what? ....
....

Biggest aggravation of the day: ....
....

I feel :

	yes	no	a bit
mellow	☐	☐	☐
peaceful	☐	☐	☐
caring	☐	☐	☐
attractive	☐	☐	☐
impressed	☐	☐	☐
honorable	☐	☐	☐
fancy	☐	☐	☐
adventurous	☐	☐	☐

	yes	no	a bit
quiet	☐	☐	☐
good	☐	☐	☐
sweet	☐	☐	☐
sassy	☐	☐	☐
productive	☐	☐	☐
phenomenal	☐	☐	☐
curious	☐	☐	☐
_____	☐	☐	☐

This made me pretty happy : ....
....

And this made me laugh : ....
....

Did I surprise myself? ☐ yes ☐ no
How so ? ....

I deserve a medal for : ....
....

Tomorrow I might : ....
....
....

Date : _____   Time : _____

I feel :

	yes	no	a bit			yes	no	a bit
------------	-----	-----	-------		--------------	-----	-----	-------
slow	☐	☐	☐		sensitive	☐	☐	☐
stubborn	☐	☐	☐		disappointed	☐	☐	☐
lonely	☐	☐	☐		fussy	☐	☐	☐
phony	☐	☐	☐		furious	☐	☐	☐
moronic	☐	☐	☐		naughty	☐	☐	☐
sharp	☐	☐	☐		haughty	☐	☐	☐
listless	☐	☐	☐		misanthropic	☐	☐	☐
antagonistic	☐	☐	☐		_____	☐	☐	☐

I felt down on my luck when : ....
....

And here's what was lacking : ....
....

I am generally ☐ unsatisfied ☐ satisfied with life because : ....
....
....

Do I wish I could be someone else? ☐ yes ☐ no
If yes, whom? ....

Am I annoyed by someone else's good mood? ☐ yes ☐ no
If yes, why? ....

This is how happy I feel:
(draw your expression)

If my mood were a color, it would be: ....

Did someone compliment me? ☐ yes ☐ no
If yes, on what? ....
And now it's time to pay myself a compliment or two!
One thing I did well: ....

.... ,

and kudos to me for ....

....

Small mishap: ....

.... ,

but here's the upside: ....

....

The three best things that happened today:
1. ....
2. ....
3. ....

Date: _____   Time: _____

Mood:

sort of OK ↑

really lousy   6 a.m.   9 a.m.   12 p.m.   3 p.m.   6 p.m.   9 p.m.   time of
                                                                       day

I didn't like this at all: ....
....
.... Oh well!

I told .... exactly what I think about
....

Now I feel ☐ better ☐ worse ☐ the same as before

Unfortunately, I wasn't able to ....
....
...., but tomorrow I'll probably manage it.

This gave me food for thought: ....
....

Suggested improvements for ☐ tomorrow ☐ the future: ....
....
....

I feel:

	yes	no	a bit			yes	no	a bit
joyful	☐	☐	☐	funny		☐	☐	☐
creative	☐	☐	☐	free		☐	☐	☐
ambitious	☐	☐	☐	dazzling		☐	☐	☐
ordinary	☐	☐	☐	clever		☐	☐	☐
alert	☐	☐	☐	efficient		☐	☐	☐
exotic	☐	☐	☐	cautious		☐	☐	☐
satisfied	☐	☐	☐	sophisticated		☐	☐	☐
mysterious	☐	☐	☐	_____		☐	☐	☐

Have I outdone myself? ☐ yes ☐ no

If yes, how? ....

....

The nicest thought of the day: ....

....

Three things that made me happy:

1. ....

2. ....

3. ....

I'm looking forward to: ....

....

Date: _____   Time: _____

I feel:

	yes	no	a bit		yes	no	a bit
bad	☐	☐	☐	gloomy	☐	☐	☐
prickly	☐	☐	☐	empty	☐	☐	☐
resigned	☐	☐	☐	indignant	☐	☐	☐
unsatisfied	☐	☐	☐	secretive	☐	☐	☐
decadent	☐	☐	☐	mild	☐	☐	☐
pensive	☐	☐	☐	_____	☐	☐	☐

This rained on my parade: ....
....

I view this as ☐ a problem ☐ a challenge, because ....
....

The future looks
☐ bleak ☐ bright ☐ filled with shimmering shades of gray

Would I rather be elsewhere right now? ☐ yes ☐ no
If yes, where and why? ....
....

The most annoying person I talked to: ....

The biggest disappointment of the day: ....
....

This is me riding the wave of success :

This was quite good : ....
....

This unfortunately less so : ....
...., but it doesn't matter.

Did I reward myself ? ☐ yes ☐ no
If yes, how and for what ? ....
....

If no, why not ? ....
....

Here's how relaxed I feel : 0% [   ] 100%

I enjoyed this : ....
....

My resolution for tomorrow : ....
....

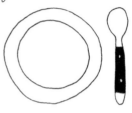

Date: _____ Time: _____

This is how much I have on my plate right now:

This put me in a really bad mood: ....
....

Especially because : ....
I would categorize the situation as a ☐ mountain ☐ molehill

I saw these people: ....
....

But I would rather have seen these people: ....
....

Three things that got on my nerves:

1. ....
2. ....
3. ....

I am this frustrated: 0% [   ] 100%

This is what I'm dreading (somewhat): ....
....

I feel:

	yes	no	a bit			yes	no	a bit
big-hearted	☐	☐	☐	patient		☐	☐	☐
gullible	☐	☐	☐	friendly		☐	☐	☐
reckless	☐	☐	☐	beloved		☐	☐	☐
cheerful	☐	☐	☐	strong		☐	☐	☐
trivial	☐	☐	☐	ethereal		☐	☐	☐
cautious	☐	☐	☐	_____		☐	☐	☐

Have I come closer to reaching my goals? ☐ yes ☐ no

How so? ....

Did I get distracted? ☐ of course not ☐ maybe a little

By what? ....

....

This couldn't have gone better: ....

....

Three things I am very satisfied with:

1. ....

2. ....

3. ....

This day was ☐ good ☐ crazy good because ....

....

....

I feel:

	yes	no	a bit			yes	no	a bit
dishonest	☐	☐	☐		restless	☐	☐	☐
static	☐	☐	☐		skeptical	☐	☐	☐
beat	☐	☐	☐		sentimental	☐	☐	☐
bored	☐	☐	☐		intelligent	☐	☐	☐
ornery	☐	☐	☐		flabbergasted	☐	☐	☐
contrite	☐	☐	☐		_____	☐	☐	☐

From the moment I woke up, I was annoyed by ....
.... Around noon,
I unfortunately ....
and in the evening I was just glad that ....
....

Anything else? ....
....
....

How well did I fail today?
☐ horribly ☐ passably ☐ brilliantly ☐ _____

What am I afraid of and why? ....
....
....

I had this many bright ideas today :
(draw a lightbulb for each idea)

Here's what I spent my time doing :

Eating : ___ hours

Sleeping : ___ hours

Reading : ___ hours

Being happy : ___ hours

Being lazy : ___ hours

_____ : ___ hours

Today, not only did I ....

....

but I also ....

....

I'm ☐ very ☐ a little bit proud of myself for it.

☐ % go-getter + ☐ % couch potato = 100% me !

This made me laugh : ....

....

This day was my friend because ....

....

....

The chaos in my head:

My head, sorted:

Date: _____ Time: _____

This is the black cat
that crossed my path:

This went awry: ....
....
....

I couldn't help but laugh, despite it all, ☐ times.
About what? ....
....
....

I frittered away quite a bit of time doing this: ....
....
....

Do I regret it? ☐ yes ☐ no

This rubbed me the wrong way: ....
....
....

Three things I could do better tomorrow:
1. ....
2. ....
3. ....

I feel:

	yes	no	a bit			yes	no	a bit
relaxed	☐	☐	☐		feisty	☐	☐	☐
perplexed	☐	☐	☐		cheeky	☐	☐	☐
chatty	☐	☐	☐		screwy	☐	☐	☐
charming	☐	☐	☐		brilliant	☐	☐	☐
exuberant	☐	☐	☐		motivated	☐	☐	☐
outgoing	☐	☐	☐	_____		☐	☐	☐

I met up with this many people: ☐ Names: ....

....

My favorite person to chat with: ....

I infected this many people with my good mood: ☐

Names: ....

What I did today to get closer to my goals: ....

....

....

Also, this happened: ....

....

....

I am excited for tomorrow, ☐ because ☐ even though ....

....

I feel:

	yes	no	a bit			yes	no	a bit
apathetic	☐	☐	☐	like a failure		☐	☐	☐
baffled	☐	☐	☐	resigned		☐	☐	☐
half-asleep	☐	☐	☐	hollow		☐	☐	☐
chaotic	☐	☐	☐	glum		☐	☐	☐
foolish	☐	☐	☐	inflexible		☐	☐	☐
lost	☐	☐	☐	_____		☐	☐	☐

I did this today: ....
....

And I would rather have done this: ....
....
....

I thought about whether I should ....
.... or not. Upon thorough reflection, I have
decided that ....
....

Do I have qualms about this? ☐ absolutely! ☐ minor ones
Why? ....
....

The lowest point of my day: ....
....
....

This is how far my leap of faith took me:

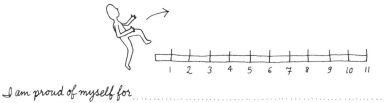

1 2 3 4 5 6 7 8 9 10 11

I am proud of myself for

This was not ideal:
but this still worked out really well:

Something that motivated me:

Three little things that brought me joy:

1.
2.
3.

I laughed ☐ times. About what?

The highlight of my day:

Date: _____   Time: _____

I've had it up to here:
(Fill in level of fed-up-ness)

This wore me out today: ....
....
....

This was running through my mind at the time: ....
....
....
....

This went very wrong: ....
....
....

How difficult is it for me to think positively right now?
☐ extremely ☐ a little bit
Why? ....
....

Some space for general griping: ....
....
....

I feel:

	yes	no	a bit			yes	no	a bit
hopeful	☐	☐	☐	refreshed	☐	☐	☐
shy	☐	☐	☐	tame	☐	☐	☐
happy	☐	☐	☐	diligent	☐	☐	☐
focused	☐	☐	☐	generous	☐	☐	☐
respectable	☐	☐	☐	unique	☐	☐	☐
unforgettable	☐	☐	☐	_____	☐	☐	☐

I didn't let this stress me out at all: ....
....

Good news: ....
....

I'm flirting with the idea of ....
....
....
....

Here's how content I am: 0% [   ] 100%

Tomorrow will be a good day because ....
....
....

Date : _____   Time : _____

I feel :

	yes	no	a bit
dreadful	☐	☐	☐
uptight	☐	☐	☐
naïve	☐	☐	☐
primitive	☐	☐	☐
bossy	☐	☐	☐
upset	☐	☐	☐
even-keeled	☐	☐	☐
taciturn	☐	☐	☐

	yes	no	a bit
stingy	☐	☐	☐
ugly	☐	☐	☐
thin-skinned	☐	☐	☐
spaced out	☐	☐	☐
superfluous	☐	☐	☐
withdrawn	☐	☐	☐
hormonal	☐	☐	☐
_____	☐	☐	☐

I would rather have done this differently : ....
....
....
....

Did I set the bar too high? ☐ yes ☐ no ☐ a bit
Details: ....
Am I plagued by doubts? ☐ yes ☐ no
Which ones? ....
It's really ☐ dramatic! ☐ not a big deal

Here's how stressed I am: 0% [_____] 100%

This is getting on my nerves: ....
....

Joy

happy
as a clam ↑

down in
the dumps

6 a.m.   9 a.m.   12 p.m.   3 p.m.   6 p.m.   9 p.m.   time of
                                                           day

Things couldn't have gone better. This morning I ....
.... , afterward I
.... and in the evening I ....
....

This exceeded my expectations as well: ....
....

Could things have gone even better? ☐ yes ☐ no ☐ maybe
How? ....
....

Did anybody make me jump for joy? ☐ yes ☐ no
Who? With what? ....
....

Here's what I wish ☐ for tomorrow ☐ for the future: ....
....
....

Aches and pains :
(mark corresponding body parts)

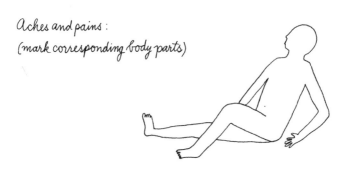

This is how much time I wasted

Working: ___ hours   Brooding: ___ hours
Eating: ___ hours   Bickering: ___ hours
Watching TV: ___ hours   _____ : ___ hours

Would I have preferred to stay in bed? ☐ yes ☐ no
Why? ....
....

My biggest fear right now is that ....
.... , but ....
....

I cried ☐ times. About what? ....
....

Biggest aggravation of the day: ....
....

I feel:

	yes	no	a bit			yes	no	a bit
mellow	☐	☐	☐	quiet	☐	☐	☐
peaceful	☐	☐	☐	good	☐	☐	☐
caring	☐	☐	☐	sweet	☐	☐	☐
attractive	☐	☐	☐	sassy	☐	☐	☐
impressed	☐	☐	☐	productive	☐	☐	☐
honorable	☐	☐	☐	phenomenal	☐	☐	☐
fancy	☐	☐	☐	curious	☐	☐	☐
adventurous	☐	☐	☐	_____	☐	☐	☐

This made me pretty happy: ....
....

And this made me laugh: ....
....

Did I surprise myself? ☐ yes ☐ no
How so? ....

I deserve a medal for: ....
....

Tomorrow I might: ....
....
....

Date: _____   Time: _____

I feel:

	yes	no	a bit			yes	no	a bit
slow	☐	☐	☐		sensitive	☐	☐	☐
stubborn	☐	☐	☐		disappointed	☐	☐	☐
lonely	☐	☐	☐		fussy	☐	☐	☐
phony	☐	☐	☐		furious	☐	☐	☐
moronic	☐	☐	☐		naughty	☐	☐	☐
sharp	☐	☐	☐		haughty	☐	☐	☐
listless	☐	☐	☐		misanthropic	☐	☐	☐
antagonistic	☐	☐	☐		_____	☐	☐	☐

I felt down on my luck when: ....
....

And here's what was lacking: ....
....

I am generally ☐ unsatisfied ☐ satisfied with life because: ....
....
....

Do I wish I could be someone else? ☐ yes ☐ no
If yes, whom? ....

Am I annoyed by someone else's good mood? ☐ yes ☐ no
If yes, why? ....

This is how happy I feel:
(draw your expression)

If my mood were a color, it would be: ....

Did someone compliment me? ☐ yes ☐ no
If yes, on what? ....
And now it's time to pay myself a compliment or two!
One thing I did well: ....

....,

and kudos to me for ....

....

Small mishap: ....

....,

but here's the upside: ....

....

The three best things that happened today:
1. ....
2. ....
3. ....

Date: _____   Time: _____

Mood:

sort of OK ↑

really lousy |___|____|____|____|____|____|____→ time of
              6 a.m. 9 a.m. 12 p.m. 3 p.m. 6 p.m. 9 p.m.   day

I didn't like this at all: ....
....
.... Oh well!

I told .... exactly what I think about
....

Now I feel ☐ better ☐ worse ☐ the same as before

Unfortunately, I wasn't able to ....
....
...., but tomorrow I'll probably manage it.

This gave me food for thought: ....
....

Suggested improvements for ☐ tomorrow ☐ the future: ....
....
....

I feel:

	yes	no	a bit
joyful	☐	☐	☐
creative	☐	☐	☐
ambitious	☐	☐	☐
ordinary	☐	☐	☐
alert	☐	☐	☐
exotic	☐	☐	☐
satisfied	☐	☐	☐
mysterious	☐	☐	☐

	yes	no	a bit
funny	☐	☐	☐
free	☐	☐	☐
dazzling	☐	☐	☐
clever	☐	☐	☐
efficient	☐	☐	☐
cautious	☐	☐	☐
sophisticated	☐	☐	☐
_____	☐	☐	☐

Have I outdone myself? ☐ yes ☐ no

If yes, how? ....

....

The nicest thought of the day: ....

....

Three things that made me happy:

1. ....

2. ....

3. ....

I'm looking forward to: ....

....

Date : _____   Time : _____

I feel :

	yes	no	a bit
bad	☐	☐	☐
prickly	☐	☐	☐
resigned	☐	☐	☐
unsatisfied	☐	☐	☐
decadent	☐	☐	☐
pensive	☐	☐	☐

	yes	no	a bit
gloomy	☐	☐	☐
empty	☐	☐	☐
indignant	☐	☐	☐
secretive	☐	☐	☐
mild	☐	☐	☐
_____	☐	☐	☐

This rained on my parade : ....
....

I view this as ☐ a problem ☐ a challenge, because ....
....

The future looks
☐ bleak ☐ bright ☐ filled with shimmering shades of gray

Would I rather be elsewhere right now? ☐ yes ☐ no
If yes, where and why? ....
....

The most annoying person I talked to : ....

The biggest disappointment of the day : ....
....

This is me riding the wave of success :

This was quite good : ....
....

This unfortunately less so : ....
...., but it doesn't matter.

Did I reward myself ? ☐ yes ☐ no
If yes, how and for what ? ....
....
If no, why not ? ....
....

Here's how relaxed I feel : 0% [   ] 100%

I enjoyed this : ....
....

My resolution for tomorrow : ....
....

Date: _____   Time: _____

This is how much I have on my plate right now:

This put me in a really bad mood: ....
....

Especially because: ....
I would categorize the situation as a ☐ mountain ☐ molehill

I saw these people: ....
....

But I would rather have seen these people: ....
....

Three things that got on my nerves:

1. ....
2. ....
3. ....

I am this frustrated: 0% [   ] 100%

This is what I'm dreading (somewhat): ....
....

I feel:

	yes	no	a bit			yes	no	a bit
big-hearted	☐	☐	☐	patient		☐	☐	☐
gullible	☐	☐	☐	friendly		☐	☐	☐
reckless	☐	☐	☐	beloved		☐	☐	☐
cheerful	☐	☐	☐	strong		☐	☐	☐
trivial	☐	☐	☐	ethereal		☐	☐	☐
cautious	☐	☐	☐	_____		☐	☐	☐

Have I come closer to reaching my goals? ☐ yes ☐ no

How so? ....

Did I get distracted? ☐ of course not ☐ maybe a little

By what? ....

....

This couldn't have gone better: ....

....

Three things I am very satisfied with:

1. ....

2. ....

3. ....

This day was ☐ good ☐ crazy good because ....

....

....

Date: _____   Time: _____

I feel:

	yes	no	a bit			yes	no	a bit
dishonest	☐	☐	☐		restless	☐	☐	☐
static	☐	☐	☐		skeptical	☐	☐	☐
beat	☐	☐	☐		sentimental	☐	☐	☐
bored	☐	☐	☐		intelligent	☐	☐	☐
ornery	☐	☐	☐		flabbergasted	☐	☐	☐
contrite	☐	☐	☐		_____	☐	☐	☐

From the moment I woke up, I was annoyed by ....
.... Around noon,
I unfortunately ....
and in the evening I was just glad that ....
....

Anything else? ....
....
....

How well did I fail today?
☐ horribly   ☐ passably   ☐ brilliantly   ☐ _____

What am I afraid of and why? ....
....
....

I had this many bright ideas today:
(draw a lightbulb for each idea)

Here's what I spent my time doing:

Eating: ___ hours

Being happy: ___ hours

Sleeping: ___ hours

Being lazy: ___ hours

Reading: ___ hours

_____: ___ hours

Today, not only did I ....

....

but I also ....

I'm ☐ very ☐ a little bit proud of myself for it.

☐% go-getter + ☐% couch potato = 100% me!

This made me laugh: ....

....

This day was my friend because ....

....

....

Date: _____   Time: _____

This is the black cat
that crossed my path:

　　　　　　　　　　　　♩♩　　　♩♩

This went awry: ....
....
....

I couldn't help but laugh, despite it all, ☐ times.
About what? ....
....
....

I frittered away quite a bit of time doing this: ....
....
....

Do I regret it? ☐ yes ☐ no

This rubbed me the wrong way: ....
....
....

Three things I could do better tomorrow:
1. ....
2. ....
3. ....

↳ I feel:

	yes	no	a bit			yes	no	a bit
relaxed	☐	☐	☐	feisty		☐	☐	☐
perplexed	☐	☐	☐	cheeky		☐	☐	☐
chatty	☐	☐	☐	screwy		☐	☐	☐
charming	☐	☐	☐	brilliant		☐	☐	☐
exuberant	☐	☐	☐	motivated		☐	☐	☐
outgoing	☐	☐	☐	_____		☐	☐	☐

I met up with this many people: ☐ Names: ....

....

My favorite person to chat with: ....

↓ I infected this many people with my good mood: ☐

Names: ....

What I did today to get closer to my goals: ....

....

....

....

Also, this happened: ....

....

....

I am excited for tomorrow, ☐ because ☐ even though ....

....

I feel:

	yes	no	a bit
apathetic	☐	☐	☐
baffled	☐	☐	☐
half-asleep	☐	☐	☐
chaotic	☐	☐	☐
foolish	☐	☐	☐
lost	☐	☐	☐

	yes	no	a bit
like a failure	☐	☐	☐
resigned	☐	☐	☐
hollow	☐	☐	☐
glum	☐	☐	☐
inflexible	☐	☐	☐
_____	☐	☐	☐

I did this today: ....
....

And I would rather have done this: ....
....
....

I thought about whether I should ....
.... or not. Upon thorough reflection, I have
decided that ....
....

Do I have qualms about this? ☐ absolutely! ☐ minor ones
Why? ....
....

The lowest point of my day: ....
....
....

This is how far my leap of faith took me :

1 2 3 4 5 6 7 8 9 10 11

I am proud of myself for ....

....

This was not ideal : ....

but this still worked out really well : ....

....

....

Something that motivated me : ....

....

Three little things that brought me joy :

1. ....

2. ....

3. ....

I laughed ⬚ times. About what ? ....

....

The highlight of my day : ....

....

....

Date: _____ Time: _____

I've had it up to here:
(Fill in level of fed-up-ness)

This wore me out today: ....
....
....

This was running through my mind at the time: ....
....
....
....

This went very wrong: ....
....
....

How difficult is it for me to think positively right now?
☐ extremely ☐ a little bit

Why? ....
....

Some space for general griping: ....
....
....

I feel:

	yes	no	a bit			yes	no	a bit
hopeful	☐	☐	☐	refreshed	☐	☐	☐
shy	☐	☐	☐	tame	☐	☐	☐
happy	☐	☐	☐	diligent	☐	☐	☐
focused	☐	☐	☐	generous	☐	☐	☐
respectable	☐	☐	☐	unique	☐	☐	☐
unforgettable	☐	☐	☐	_____	☐	☐	☐

I didn't let this stress me out at all: ....

....

Good news: ....

....

I'm flirting with the idea of ....

....

....

....

Here's how content I am: 0% [   ] 100%

Tomorrow will be a good day because ....

....

....

I feel :

	yes	no	a bit
dreadful	☐	☐	☐
uptight	☐	☐	☐
naïve	☐	☐	☐
primitive	☐	☐	☐
bossy	☐	☐	☐
upset	☐	☐	☐
even-keeled	☐	☐	☐
taciturn	☐	☐	☐

	yes	no	a bit
stingy	☐	☐	☐
ugly	☐	☐	☐
thin-skinned	☐	☐	☐
spaced out	☐	☐	☐
superfluous	☐	☐	☐
withdrawn	☐	☐	☐
hormonal	☐	☐	☐
_____	☐	☐	☐

I would rather have done this differently : ....
....
....
....

Did I set the bar too high? ☐ yes ☐ no ☐ a bit
Details : ....
Am I plagued by doubts? ☐ yes ☐ no
Which ones? ....
It's really ☐ dramatic! ☐ not a big deal

Here's how stressed I am: 0% [   ] 100%

This is getting on my nerves: ....
....

Joy

happy as a clam ↑

down in the dumps

6 a.m.   9 a.m.   12 p.m.   3 p.m.   6 p.m.   9 p.m.   time of day →

Things couldn't have gone better. This morning I ....
...., afterward I
.... and in the evening I ....
....

This exceeded my expectations as well: ....
....

Could things have gone even better? ☐ yes ☐ no ☐ maybe
How? ....
....

Did anybody make me jump for joy? ☐ yes ☐ no
Who? With what? ....
....

Here's what I wish ☐ for tomorrow ☐ for the future: ....
....
....

Date: _____ Time: _____

Aches and pains:
(mark corresponding body parts)

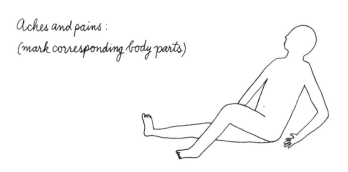

This is how much time I wasted
Working: __ hours   Brooding: __ hours
Eating: __ hours   Bickering: __ hours
Watching TV: __ hours   _____: __ hours

Would I have preferred to stay in bed? ☐ yes ☐ no
Why? ....
....

My biggest fear right now is that ....
...., but ....
....

I cried ☐ times. About what? ....
....

Biggest aggravation of the day: ....
....

I feel:

	yes	no	a bit
mellow	☐	☐	☐
peaceful	☐	☐	☐
caring	☐	☐	☐
attractive	☐	☐	☐
impressed	☐	☐	☐
honorable	☐	☐	☐
fancy	☐	☐	☐
adventurous	☐	☐	☐

	yes	no	a bit
quiet	☐	☐	☐
good	☐	☐	☐
sweet	☐	☐	☐
sassy	☐	☐	☐
productive	☐	☐	☐
phenomenal	☐	☐	☐
curious	☐	☐	☐
_____	☐	☐	☐

This made me pretty happy: ....
....

And this made me laugh: ....
....

Did I surprise myself? ☐ yes ☐ no
How so? ....

I deserve a medal for: ....
....

Tomorrow I might: ....
....
....

Date: _____   Time: _____

I feel:

	yes	no	a bit			yes	no	a bit
slow	☐	☐	☐		sensitive	☐	☐	☐
stubborn	☐	☐	☐		disappointed	☐	☐	☐
lonely	☐	☐	☐		fussy	☐	☐	☐
phony	☐	☐	☐		furious	☐	☐	☐
moronic	☐	☐	☐		naughty	☐	☐	☐
sharp	☐	☐	☐		haughty	☐	☐	☐
listless	☐	☐	☐		misanthropic	☐	☐	☐
antagonistic	☐	☐	☐		_____	☐	☐	☐

I felt down on my luck when: ....
....

And here's what was lacking: ....
....

I am generally ☐ unsatisfied ☐ satisfied with life because: ....
....
....

Do I wish I could be someone else? ☐ yes ☐ no
If yes, whom? ....

Am I annoyed by someone else's good mood? ☐ yes ☐ no
If yes, why? ....

This is how happy I feel:
(draw your expression)

If my mood were a color, it would be: ....

Did someone compliment me? ☐ yes ☐ no
If yes, on what? ....
And now it's time to pay myself a compliment or two!
One thing I did well: ....

....)

and kudos to me for ....

....

Small mishap: ....

....)

but here's the upside: ....

....

The three best things that happened today:
1. ....
2. ....
3. ....

Date: _____ Time: _____

Mood:

sort of OK ↑

really lousy └─┬────┬────┬────┬────┬────┬──→ time of
             6 a.m. 9 a.m. 12 p.m. 3 p.m. 6 p.m. 9 p.m. day

I didn't like this at all: ....
....
.... Oh well!

I told .... exactly what I think about
....

Now I feel ☐ better ☐ worse ☐ the same as before

Unfortunately, I wasn't able to ....
....
....................................), but tomorrow I'll probably manage it.

This gave me food for thought: ....
....

Suggested improvements for ☐ tomorrow ☐ the future: ....
....
....

I feel:

	yes	no	a bit			yes	no	a bit
joyful	☐	☐	☐		funny	☐	☐	☐
creative	☐	☐	☐		free	☐	☐	☐
ambitious	☐	☐	☐		dazzling	☐	☐	☐
ordinary	☐	☐	☐		clever	☐	☐	☐
alert	☐	☐	☐		efficient	☐	☐	☐
exotic	☐	☐	☐		cautious	☐	☐	☐
satisfied	☐	☐	☐		sophisticated	☐	☐	☐
mysterious	☐	☐	☐		_____	☐	☐	☐

Have I outdone myself? ☐ yes ☐ no

If yes, how? ....
....

The nicest thought of the day: ....
....

Three things that made me happy:

1. ....
2. ....
3. ....

I'm looking forward to: ....
....

Date: _____ Time: _____

I feel:

	yes	no	a bit			yes	no	a bit
bad	☐	☐	☐	gloomy	☐	☐	☐
prickly	☐	☐	☐	empty	☐	☐	☐
resigned	☐	☐	☐	indignant	☐	☐	☐
unsatisfied	☐	☐	☐	secretive	☐	☐	☐
decadent	☐	☐	☐	mild	☐	☐	☐
pensive	☐	☐	☐	_____	☐	☐	☐

This rained on my parade : ....
....

I view this as ☐ a problem ☐ a challenge, because ....
....

The future looks
☐ bleak ☐ bright ☐ filled with shimmering shades of gray

Would I rather be elsewhere right now? ☐ yes ☐ no
If yes, where and why? ....
....

The most annoying person I talked to: ....

The biggest disappointment of the day: ....
....

This is me riding the wave of success:

This was quite good: ....
....
This unfortunately less so: ....
...., but it doesn't matter.

Did I reward myself? ☐ yes ☐ no
If yes, how and for what? ....
....
If no, why not? ....
....

Here's how relaxed I feel: 0% [   ] 100%

I enjoyed this: ....
....

My resolution for tomorrow: ....
....

Date: _____ Time: _____

This is how much I have on my plate right now:

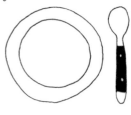

This put me in a really bad mood: ....
....

Especially because: ....
I would categorize the situation as a ☐ mountain ☐ molehill

I saw these people: ....
....

But I would rather have seen these people: ....
....

Three things that got on my nerves:

1. ....
2. ....
3. ....

I am this frustrated: 0% [_____] 100%

This is what I'm dreading (somewhat): ....
....

I feel:

	yes	no	a bit		yes	no	a bit
big-hearted	☐	☐	☐	patient	☐	☐	☐
gullible	☐	☐	☐	friendly	☐	☐	☐
reckless	☐	☐	☐	beloved	☐	☐	☐
cheerful	☐	☐	☐	strong	☐	☐	☐
trivial	☐	☐	☐	ethereal	☐	☐	☐
cautious	☐	☐	☐	_____	☐	☐	☐

Have I come closer to reaching my goals? ☐ yes ☐ no

How so? ....

Did I get distracted? ☐ of course not ☐ maybe a little

By what? ....

....

This couldn't have gone better: ....

....

Three things I am very satisfied with:

1. ....

2. ....

3. ....

This day was ☐ good ☐ crazy good because ....

....

....

Date: _____ Time: _____

I feel:

	yes	no	a bit			yes	no	a bit
dishonest	☐	☐	☐	restless		☐	☐	☐
static	☐	☐	☐	skeptical		☐	☐	☐
beat	☐	☐	☐	sentimental		☐	☐	☐
bored	☐	☐	☐	intelligent		☐	☐	☐
ornery	☐	☐	☐	flabbergasted		☐	☐	☐
contrite	☐	☐	☐	_____		☐	☐	☐

From the moment I woke up, I was annoyed by ....
.... Around noon,
I unfortunately ....
and in the evening I was just glad that ....
....

Anything else? ....
....
....

How well did I fail today?
☐ horribly ☐ passably ☐ brilliantly ☐ _____

What am I afraid of and why? ....
....
....

I had this many bright ideas today:
(draw a lightbulb for each idea)

Here's what I spent my time doing:

Eating: __ hours

Sleeping: __ hours

Reading: __ hours

Being happy: __ hours

Being lazy: __ hours

_____: __ hours

Today, not only did I ....

but I also ....

I'm ☐ very ☐ a little bit proud of myself for it.

☐ % go-getter + ☐ % couch potato = 100% me!

This made me laugh: ....

....

This day was my friend because ....

....

....

Rough Seas
(draw the stormy weather)

This is going off-course at the moment : ....
....
....
....
....
....
....
....
....
....
....

Wind in My Sails
(draw the beautiful weather)

This is going great right now:

Date: _____   Time: _____

This is the black cat
that crossed my path:

This went awry: ....
....
....

I couldn't help but laugh, despite it all, ☐ times.
About what? ....
....
....

I frittered away quite a bit of time doing this: ....
....
....

Do I regret it? ☐ yes ☐ no

This rubbed me the wrong way: ....
....
....

Three things I could do better tomorrow:
1. ....
2. ....
3. ....

I feel:

	yes	no	a bit			yes	no	a bit
relaxed	☐	☐	☐	feisty		☐	☐	☐
perplexed	☐	☐	☐	cheeky		☐	☐	☐
chatty	☐	☐	☐	screwy		☐	☐	☐
charming	☐	☐	☐	brilliant		☐	☐	☐
exuberant	☐	☐	☐	motivated		☐	☐	☐
outgoing	☐	☐	☐	___		☐	☐	☐

I met up with this many people: ☐ Names: ....
....

My favorite person to chat with: ....
I infected this many people with my good mood: ☐
Names: ....

What I did today to get closer to my goals: ....
....
....

Also, this happened: ....
....
....

I am excited for tomorrow, ☐ because ☐ even though ....
....

Date: _____   Time: _____

I feel:

	yes	no	a bit		yes	no	a bit
apathetic	☐	☐	☐	like a failure	☐	☐	☐
baffled	☐	☐	☐	resigned	☐	☐	☐
half-asleep	☐	☐	☐	hollow	☐	☐	☐
chaotic	☐	☐	☐	glum	☐	☐	☐
foolish	☐	☐	☐	inflexible	☐	☐	☐
lost	☐	☐	☐	_____	☐	☐	☐

I did this today: ....

....

And I would rather have done this: ....

....

....

I thought about whether I should ....

.... or not. Upon thorough reflection, I have

decided that ....

....

Do I have qualms about this? ☐ absolutely! ☐ minor ones

Why? ....

....

The lowest point of my day: ....

....

....

This is how far my leap of faith took me:

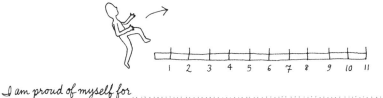

1 2 3 4 5 6 7 8 9 10 11

I am proud of myself for ....

....

This was not ideal: ....

but this still worked out really well: ....

....

....

Something that motivated me: ....

....

Three little things that brought me joy:

1. ....

2. ....

3. ....

I laughed ☐ times. About what? ....

....

The highlight of my day: ....

....

....

Date: _____   Time: _____

I've had it up to here:
(Fill in level of fed-up-ness)

This wore me out today: ....
....
....

This was running through my mind at the time: ....
....
....
....

This went very wrong: ....
....
....

How difficult is it for me to think positively right now?
☐ extremely ☐ a little bit
Why? ....
....

Some space for general griping: ....
....
....

I feel:

	yes	no	a bit			yes	no	a bit
hopeful	☐	☐	☐	refreshed	☐	☐	☐
shy	☐	☐	☐	tame	☐	☐	☐
happy	☐	☐	☐	diligent	☐	☐	☐
focused	☐	☐	☐	generous	☐	☐	☐
respectable	☐	☐	☐	unique	☐	☐	☐
unforgettable	☐	☐	☐	_____	☐	☐	☐

I didn't let this stress me out at all: ....

....

Good news: ....

....

I'm flirting with the idea of ....

....

....

....

Here's how content I am: 0% [   ] 100%

Tomorrow will be a good day because ....

....

....

Date: _____ Time: _____

I feel:

	yes	no	a bit			yes	no	a bit
dreadful	☐	☐	☐	stingy		☐	☐	☐
uptight	☐	☐	☐	ugly		☐	☐	☐
naïve	☐	☐	☐	thin-skinned		☐	☐	☐
primitive	☐	☐	☐	spaced out		☐	☐	☐
bossy	☐	☐	☐	superfluous		☐	☐	☐
upset	☐	☐	☐	withdrawn		☐	☐	☐
even-keeled	☐	☐	☐	hormonal		☐	☐	☐
taciturn	☐	☐	☐	_____		☐	☐	☐

I would rather have done this differently : ....
....
....
....

Did I set the bar too high? ☐ yes ☐ no ☐ a bit
Details: ....
Am I plagued by doubts? ☐ yes ☐ no
Which ones? ....
It's really ☐ dramatic! ☐ not a big deal

Here's how stressed I am: 0% [_____] 100%

This is getting on my nerves: ....
....

Joy

happy
as a clam

down in
the dumps

6 a.m.   9 a.m.   12 p.m.   3 p.m.   6 p.m.   9 p.m.   time of
                                                                  day

Things couldn't have gone better. This morning I ....
.... , afterward I
.... and in the evening I ....
....

This exceeded my expectations as well: ....
....

Could things have gone even better? ☐ yes ☐ no ☐ maybe
How? ....
....

Did anybody make me jump for joy? ☐ yes ☐ no
Who? With what? ....
....

Here's what I wish ☐ for tomorrow ☐ for the future: ....
....
....

Aches and pains :
(mark corresponding body parts)

This is how much time I wasted

Working: __ hours   Brooding: __ hours

Eating: __ hours   Bickering: __ hours

Watching TV: __ hours   _____: __ hours

Would I have preferred to stay in bed? ☐ yes ☐ no

Why? ....

....

My biggest fear right now is that ....

.... , but ....

....

I cried ☐ times. About what? ....

....

Biggest aggravation of the day: ....

....

I feel:

	yes	no	a bit			yes	no	a bit
mellow	☐	☐	☐	quiet	☐	☐	☐
peaceful	☐	☐	☐	good	☐	☐	☐
caring	☐	☐	☐	sweet	☐	☐	☐
attractive	☐	☐	☐	sassy	☐	☐	☐
impressed	☐	☐	☐	productive	☐	☐	☐
honorable	☐	☐	☐	phenomenal	☐	☐	☐
fancy	☐	☐	☐	curious	☐	☐	☐
adventurous	☐	☐	☐	_____	☐	☐	☐

This made me pretty happy: ....
....

And this made me laugh: ....
....

Did I surprise myself? ☐ yes ☐ no
How so? ....

I deserve a medal for: ....
....

Tomorrow I might: ....
....
....

Date: _____   Time: _____

I feel:

	yes	no	a bit			yes	no	a bit
slow	☐	☐	☐		sensitive	☐	☐	☐
stubborn	☐	☐	☐		disappointed	☐	☐	☐
lonely	☐	☐	☐		fussy	☐	☐	☐
phony	☐	☐	☐		furious	☐	☐	☐
moronic	☐	☐	☐		naughty	☐	☐	☐
sharp	☐	☐	☐		haughty	☐	☐	☐
listless	☐	☐	☐		misanthropic	☐	☐	☐
antagonistic	☐	☐	☐		_____	☐	☐	☐

I felt down on my luck when: ....
....

And here's what was lacking: ....
....

I am generally ☐ unsatisfied ☐ satisfied with life because: ....
....
....

Do I wish I could be someone else? ☐ yes ☐ no
If yes, whom? ....

Am I annoyed by someone else's good mood? ☐ yes ☐ no
If yes, why? ....

This is how happy I feel :
(draw your expression)

If my mood were a color, it would be : ....

Did someone compliment me? ☐ yes ☐ no
If yes, on what? ....
And now it's time to pay myself a compliment or two!
One thing I did well : ....

....)

and kudos to me for ....

....

Small mishap : ....

....)

but here's the upside : ....

....

The three best things that happened today :
1 ....
2 ....
3 ....

Date : _____   Time : _____

Mood :

I didn't like this at all : ....
....
.... Oh well !

I told .... exactly what I think about

....

Now I feel ☐ better ☐ worse ☐ the same as before

Unfortunately, I wasn't able to ....

....

.................................., but tomorrow I'll probably manage it.

This gave me food for thought : ....

....

Suggested improvements for ☐ tomorrow ☐ the future : ....

....

....

I feel:

	yes	no	a bit			yes	no	a bit
joyful	☐	☐	☐	funny		☐	☐	☐
creative	☐	☐	☐	free		☐	☐	☐
ambitious	☐	☐	☐	dazzling		☐	☐	☐
ordinary	☐	☐	☐	clever		☐	☐	☐
alert	☐	☐	☐	efficient		☐	☐	☐
exotic	☐	☐	☐	cautious		☐	☐	☐
satisfied	☐	☐	☐	sophisticated		☐	☐	☐
mysterious	☐	☐	☐	_____		☐	☐	☐

Have I outdone myself? ☐ yes ☐ no

If yes, how? ....
....

The nicest thought of the day: ....
....

Three things that made me happy:

1. ....
2. ....
3. ....

I'm looking forward to: ....
....

Date: _____ Time: _____

I feel:

	yes	no	a bit			yes	no	a bit
bad	☐	☐	☐	gloomy	☐	☐	☐
prickly	☐	☐	☐	empty	☐	☐	☐
resigned	☐	☐	☐	indignant	☐	☐	☐
unsatisfied	☐	☐	☐	secretive	☐	☐	☐
decadent	☐	☐	☐	mild	☐	☐	☐
pensive	☐	☐	☐	_____	☐	☐	☐

This rained on my parade: ....
....

I view this as ☐ a problem ☐ a challenge, because ....
....

The future looks
☐ bleak ☐ bright ☐ filled with shimmering shades of gray

Would I rather be elsewhere right now? ☐ yes ☐ no
If yes, where and why? ....
....

The most annoying person I talked to: ....

The biggest disappointment of the day: ....
....

This is me riding the wave of success :

This was quite good : ....
....
This unfortunately less so : ....
...., but it doesn't matter.

Did I reward myself ? ☐ yes ☐ no
If yes, how and for what ? ....
....
If no, why not ? ....
....

Here's how relaxed I feel : 0% [   ] 100%

I enjoyed this : ....
....

My resolution for tomorrow : ....
....

Date: _____   Time: _____

This is how much I have on my plate right now:

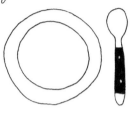

This put me in a really bad mood: ....
....

Especially because: ....
I would categorize the situation as a ☐ mountain ☐ molehill

I saw these people: ....
....

But I would rather have seen these people: ....
....

Three things that got on my nerves:

1. ....
2. ....
3. ....

I am this frustrated: 0% [_____] 100%

This is what I'm dreading (somewhat): ....
....

I feel:

	yes	no	a bit			yes	no	a bit
big-hearted	☐	☐	☐	patient		☐	☐	☐
gullible	☐	☐	☐	friendly		☐	☐	☐
reckless	☐	☐	☐	beloved		☐	☐	☐
cheerful	☐	☐	☐	strong		☐	☐	☐
trivial	☐	☐	☐	ethereal		☐	☐	☐
cautious	☐	☐	☐	_____		☐	☐	☐

Have I come closer to reaching my goals? ☐ yes ☐ no

How so? ....

Did I get distracted? ☐ of course not ☐ maybe a little

By what? ....

....

This couldn't have gone better: ....

....

Three things I am very satisfied with:

1. ....

2. ....

3. ....

This day was ☐ good ☐ crazy good because ....

....

....

Date: _____ Time: _____

I feel:

	yes	no	a bit			yes	no	a bit
dishonest	☐	☐	☐	restless		☐	☐	☐
static	☐	☐	☐	skeptical		☐	☐	☐
beat	☐	☐	☐	sentimental		☐	☐	☐
bored	☐	☐	☐	intelligent		☐	☐	☐
ornery	☐	☐	☐	flabbergasted		☐	☐	☐
contrite	☐	☐	☐	_____		☐	☐	☐

From the moment I woke up, I was annoyed by ....
.... Around noon,
I unfortunately ....
and in the evening I was just glad that ....
....

Anything else? ....
....
....

How well did I fail today?
☐ horribly ☐ passably ☐ brilliantly ☐ _____

What am I afraid of and why? ....
....
....

I had this many bright ideas today:
(draw a lightbulb for each idea)

Here's what I spent my time doing:

Eating: ___ hours

Being happy: ___ hours

Sleeping: ___ hours

Being lazy: ___ hours

Reading: ___ hours

_____ : ___ hours

Today, not only did I ....

but I also ....

I'm ☐ very ☐ a little bit proud of myself for it.

☐ % go-getter + ☐ % couch potato = 100% me!

This made me laugh: ....

....

This day was my friend because ....

....

....

Date : _____   Time : _____

This is the black cat
that crossed my path :

This went awry : ....
....
....

I couldn't help but laugh, despite it all, ☐ times.
About what ? ....
....
....

I frittered away quite a bit of time doing this : ....
....
....

Do I regret it? ☐ yes ☐ no

This rubbed me the wrong way : ....
....
....

Three things I could do better tomorrow :
1. ....
2. ....
3. ....

→ I feel:

	yes	no	a bit
relaxed	☐	☐	☐
perplexed	☐	☐	☐
chatty	☐	☐	☐
charming	☐	☐	☐
exuberant	☐	☐	☐
outgoing	☐	☐	☐

	yes	no	a bit
feisty	☐	☐	☐
cheeky	☐	☐	☐
screwy	☐	☐	☐
brilliant	☐	☐	☐
motivated	☐	☐	☐
_____	☐	☐	☐

I met up with this many people: ☐ Names: ....
....

My favorite person to chat with: ....
I infected this many people with my good mood: ☐
Names: ....

What I did today to get closer to my goals: ....
....
....
....

Also, this happened: ....
....
....

I am excited for tomorrow, ☐ because ☐ even though ....
....

Date: _____   Time: _____

I feel:

	yes	no	a bit			yes	no	a bit
apathetic	☐	☐	☐	like a failure	☐	☐	☐
baffled	☐	☐	☐	resigned	☐	☐	☐
half-asleep	☐	☐	☐	hollow	☐	☐	☐
chaotic	☐	☐	☐	glum	☐	☐	☐
foolish	☐	☐	☐	inflexible	☐	☐	☐
lost	☐	☐	☐	_____	☐	☐	☐

I did this today: ....
....

And I would rather have done this: ....
....
....

I thought about whether I should ....
.... or not. Upon thorough reflection, I have
decided that ....
....

Do I have qualms about this? ☐ absolutely! ☐ minor ones
Why? ....
....

The lowest point of my day: ....
....
....

This is how far my leap of faith took me:

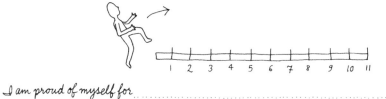

1 2 3 4 5 6 7 8 9 10 11

I am proud of myself for ....

....

This was not ideal: ....

but this still worked out really well: ....

....

....

Something that motivated me: ....

....

Three little things that brought me joy:

1. ....

2. ....

3. ....

I laughed ☐ times. About what? ....

....

The highlight of my day: ....

....

....

Date: _____ Time: _____

I've had it up to here:
(Fill in level of fed-up-ness)

This wore me out today: ....
....
....

This was running through my mind at the time: ....
....
....

This went very wrong: ....
....
....

How difficult is it for me to think positively right now?
☐ extremely ☐ a little bit
Why? ....
....

Some space for general griping: ....
....
....

I feel:

	yes	no	a bit			yes	no	a bit
hopeful	☐	☐	☐	refreshed	☐	☐	☐
shy	☐	☐	☐	tame	☐	☐	☐
happy	☐	☐	☐	diligent	☐	☐	☐
focused	☐	☐	☐	generous	☐	☐	☐
respectable	☐	☐	☐	unique	☐	☐	☐
unforgettable	☐	☐	☐	_____	☐	☐	☐

I didn't let this stress me out at all: ....
....

Good news: ....
....

I'm flirting with the idea of ....
....
....
....

Here's how content I am: 0% [   ] 100%

Tomorrow will be a good day because ....
....
....

Date: _____   Time: _____

I feel:

	yes	no	a bit		yes	no	a bit
dreadful	☐	☐	☐	stingy	☐	☐	☐
uptight	☐	☐	☐	ugly	☐	☐	☐
naïve	☐	☐	☐	thin-skinned	☐	☐	☐
primitive	☐	☐	☐	spaced out	☐	☐	☐
bossy	☐	☐	☐	superfluous	☐	☐	☐
upset	☐	☐	☐	withdrawn	☐	☐	☐
even-keeled	☐	☐	☐	hormonal	☐	☐	☐
taciturn	☐	☐	☐	_____	☐	☐	☐

I would rather have done this differently: ....
....
....
....

Did I set the bar too high? ☐ yes ☐ no ☐ a bit
Details: ....
Am I plagued by doubts? ☐ yes ☐ no
Which ones? ....
It's really ☐ dramatic! ☐ not a big deal

Here's how stressed I am: 0% [_____] 100%

This is getting on my nerves: ....
....

Joy

happy
as a clam ↑

down in
the dumps

6 a.m.   9 a.m.   12 p.m.   3 p.m.   6 p.m.   9 p.m.   time of
day

Things couldn't have gone better. This morning I ....
.... , afterward I
.... and in the evening I ....
....

This exceeded my expectations as well: ....
....

Could things have gone even better? ☐ yes ☐ no ☐ maybe
How? ....
....

Did anybody make me jump for joy? ☐ yes ☐ no
Who? With what? ....
....

Here's what I wish ☐ for tomorrow ☐ for the future: ....
....
....

Date : _____   Time : _____

Aches and pains :
(mark corresponding body parts)

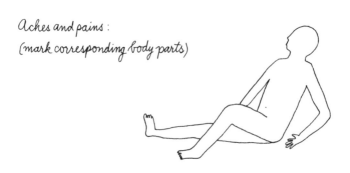

This is how much time I wasted

Working: __ hours   Brooding: __ hours
Eating: __ hours   Bickering: __ hours
Watching TV: __ hours   _____: __ hours

Would I have preferred to stay in bed? ☐ yes ☐ no
Why? ....
....

My biggest fear right now is that ....
.... , but ....
....

I cried ☐ times. About what? ....
....

Biggest aggravation of the day: ....
....

I feel:

	yes	no	a bit
mellow	☐	☐	☐
peaceful	☐	☐	☐
caring	☐	☐	☐
attractive	☐	☐	☐
impressed	☐	☐	☐
honorable	☐	☐	☐
fancy	☐	☐	☐
adventurous	☐	☐	☐

	yes	no	a bit
quiet	☐	☐	☐
good	☐	☐	☐
sweet	☐	☐	☐
sassy	☐	☐	☐
productive	☐	☐	☐
phenomenal	☐	☐	☐
curious	☐	☐	☐
_____	☐	☐	☐

This made me pretty happy: ....
....

And this made me laugh: ....
....

Did I surprise myself? ☐ yes ☐ no
How so? ....

I deserve a medal for: ....
....

Tomorrow I might: ....
....
....

Date: _____ **Time:** _____

I feel:

	yes	no	a bit			yes	no	a bit
slow	☐	☐	☐		sensitive	☐	☐	☐
stubborn	☐	☐	☐		disappointed	☐	☐	☐
lonely	☐	☐	☐		fussy	☐	☐	☐
phony	☐	☐	☐		furious	☐	☐	☐
moronic	☐	☐	☐		naughty	☐	☐	☐
sharp	☐	☐	☐		haughty	☐	☐	☐
listless	☐	☐	☐		misanthropic	☐	☐	☐
antagonistic	☐	☐	☐		_____	☐	☐	☐

I felt down on my luck when: ....

....

And here's what was lacking: ....

....

I am generally ☐ unsatisfied ☐ satisfied with life because: ....

....

....

Do I wish I could be someone else? ☐ yes ☐ no

If yes, whom? ....

Am I annoyed by someone else's good mood? ☐ yes ☐ no

If yes, why? ....

This is how happy I feel:
(draw your expression)

If my mood were a color, it would be: ....

Did someone compliment me? ☐ yes ☐ no
If yes, on what? ....
And now it's time to pay myself a compliment or two!
One thing I did well: ....

....)

and kudos to me for ....

....

Small mishap: ....

....)

but here's the upside: ....

....

The three best things that happened today:
1. ....
2. ....
3. ....

Date: _____ **Time:** _____

Mood:

sort of OK ↑

really lousy

6 a.m.　9 a.m.　12 p.m.　3 p.m.　6 p.m.　9 p.m.　time of day

I didn't like this at all: ....
....
.... Oh well!

I told .... exactly what I think about
....

Now I feel ☐ better ☐ worse ☐ the same as before

Unfortunately, I wasn't able to ....
....
...., but tomorrow I'll probably manage it.

This gave me food for thought: ....
....

Suggested improvements for ☐ tomorrow ☐ the future: ....
....
....

I feel:

	yes	no	a bit			yes	no	a bit
joyful	☐	☐	☐	funny		☐	☐	☐
creative	☐	☐	☐	free		☐	☐	☐
ambitious	☐	☐	☐	dazzling		☐	☐	☐
ordinary	☐	☐	☐	clever		☐	☐	☐
alert	☐	☐	☐	efficient		☐	☐	☐
exotic	☐	☐	☐	cautious		☐	☐	☐
satisfied	☐	☐	☐	sophisticated		☐	☐	☐
mysterious	☐	☐	☐	_____		☐	☐	☐

Have I outdone myself? ☐ yes ☐ no

If yes, how? ....

....

The nicest thought of the day: ....

....

Three things that made me happy:

1. ....

2. ....

3. ....

I'm looking forward to: ....

....

Date: _____   Time: _____

I feel:

	yes	no	a bit			yes	no	a bit
bad	☐	☐	☐	gloomy	☐	☐	☐
prickly	☐	☐	☐	empty	☐	☐	☐
resigned	☐	☐	☐	indignant	☐	☐	☐
unsatisfied	☐	☐	☐	secretive	☐	☐	☐
decadent	☐	☐	☐	mild	☐	☐	☐
pensive	☐	☐	☐	_____	☐	☐	☐

This rained on my parade: ....
....

I view this as ☐ a problem ☐ a challenge, because ....
....

The future looks
☐ bleak ☐ bright ☐ filled with shimmering shades of gray

Would I rather be elsewhere right now? ☐ yes ☐ no
If yes, where and why? ....
....

The most annoying person I talked to: ....

The biggest disappointment of the day: ....
....

This is me riding the wave of success :

This was quite good : ....
....

This unfortunately less so : ....
...., but it doesn't matter.

Did I reward myself ? ☐ yes ☐ no
If yes, how and for what ? ....
....

If no, why not ? ....
....

Here's how relaxed I feel : 0% [   ] 100%

I enjoyed this : ....
....

My resolution for tomorrow : ....
....

Date: _____   Time: _____

This is how much I have on my plate right now:

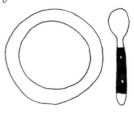

This put me in a really bad mood: ....
....

Especially because: ....
I would categorize the situation as a ☐ mountain ☐ molehill

I saw these people: ....
....

But I would rather have seen these people: ....
....

Three things that got on my nerves:
1. ....
2. ....
3. ....

I am this frustrated: 0% [_____] 100%

This is what I'm dreading (somewhat): ....
....

I feel:

	yes	no	a bit		yes	no	a bit
big-hearted	☐	☐	☐	patient	☐	☐	☐
gullible	☐	☐	☐	friendly	☐	☐	☐
reckless	☐	☐	☐	beloved	☐	☐	☐
cheerful	☐	☐	☐	strong	☐	☐	☐
trivial	☐	☐	☐	ethereal	☐	☐	☐
cautious	☐	☐	☐	————	☐	☐	☐

Have I come closer to reaching my goals? ☐ yes ☐ no

How so? ....

Did I get distracted? ☐ of course not ☐ maybe a little

By what? ....

....

This couldn't have gone better: ....

....

Three things I am very satisfied with:

1. ....

2. ....

3. ....

This day was ☐ good ☐ crazy good because ....

....

....

Date: _____   Time: _____

I feel:

	yes	no	a bit			yes	no	a bit
dishonest	☐	☐	☐		restless	☐	☐	☐
static	☐	☐	☐		skeptical	☐	☐	☐
beat	☐	☐	☐		sentimental	☐	☐	☐
bored	☐	☐	☐		intelligent	☐	☐	☐
ornery	☐	☐	☐		flabbergasted	☐	☐	☐
contrite	☐	☐	☐		_____	☐	☐	☐

From the moment I woke up, I was annoyed by ....
.... Around noon,
I unfortunately ....
and in the evening I was just glad that ....
....

Anything else? ....
....
....

How well did I fail today?
☐ horribly ☐ passably ☐ brilliantly ☐ _____

What am I afraid of and why? ....
....
....

I had this many bright ideas today:
(draw a lightbulb for each idea)

Here's what I spent my time doing:

Eating: ___ hours   Being happy: ___ hours
Sleeping: ___ hours   Being lazy: ___ hours
Reading: ___ hours   _____: ___ hours

Today, not only did I ....
....

but I also ....
....

I'm ☐ very ☐ a little bit proud of myself for it.

☐ % go-getter + ☐ % couch potato = 100% me!

This made me laugh: ....
....

This day was my friend because ....
....
....

Date: _____   Time: _____

This is the black cat
that crossed my path:

𝅘𝅥 𝅘𝅥   𝅘𝅥 𝅘𝅥

This went awry: ....
....
....

I couldn't help but laugh, despite it all, ☐ times.
About what? ....
....
....

I frittered away quite a bit of time doing this: ....
....
....

Do I regret it? ☐ yes ☐ no

This rubbed me the wrong way: ....
....
....

Three things I could do better tomorrow:
1. ....
2. ....
3. ....

I feel:

	yes	no	a bit			yes	no	a bit
relaxed	☐	☐	☐	feisty		☐	☐	☐
perplexed	☐	☐	☐	cheeky		☐	☐	☐
chatty	☐	☐	☐	screwy		☐	☐	☐
charming	☐	☐	☐	brilliant		☐	☐	☐
exuberant	☐	☐	☐	motivated		☐	☐	☐
outgoing	☐	☐	☐	_____		☐	☐	☐

I met up with this many people: ☐ Names: ....

....

My favorite person to chat with: ....

I infected this many people with my good mood: ☐

Names: ....

What I did today to get closer to my goals: ....

....

....

....

Also, this happened: ....

....

....

I am excited for tomorrow, ☐ because ☐ even though ....

....

Date: _____   Time: _____

I feel:

	yes	no	a bit
apathetic	☐	☐	☐
baffled	☐	☐	☐
half-asleep	☐	☐	☐
chaotic	☐	☐	☐
foolish	☐	☐	☐
lost	☐	☐	☐

	yes	no	a bit
like a failure	☐	☐	☐
resigned	☐	☐	☐
hollow	☐	☐	☐
glum	☐	☐	☐
inflexible	☐	☐	☐
_____	☐	☐	☐

I did this today: ....
....

And I would rather have done this: ....
....
....

I thought about whether I should ....
.... or not. Upon thorough reflection, I have

decided that ....
....

Do I have qualms about this? ☐ absolutely! ☐ minor ones

Why? ....
....

The lowest point of my day: ....
....
....

This is how far my leap of faith took me:

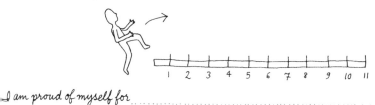

I am proud of myself for ....

This was not ideal: ....

but this still worked out really well: ....

....

Something that motivated me: ....

....

Three little things that brought me joy:

1. ....

2. ....

3. ....

I laughed ☐ times. About what? ....

....

The highlight of my day: ....

....

....

<u>Date :</u>   Time :

I've had it up to here :
(Fill in level of fed-up-ness)

This wore me out today : ....
....
....

This was running through my mind at the time : ....
....
....
....

This went very wrong : ....
....
....

How difficult is it for me to think positively right now ?
☐ extremely ☐ a little bit
Why ? ....
....

Some space for general griping : ....
....
....

I feel:

	yes	no	a bit			yes	no	a bit
hopeful	☐	☐	☐	refreshed		☐	☐	☐
shy	☐	☐	☐	tame		☐	☐	☐
happy	☐	☐	☐	diligent		☐	☐	☐
focused	☐	☐	☐	generous		☐	☐	☐
respectable	☐	☐	☐	unique		☐	☐	☐
unforgettable	☐	☐	☐	_____		☐	☐	☐

I didn't let this stress me out at all: ....
....
....

Good news: ....
....

I'm flirting with the idea of ....
....
....
....

Here's how content I am: 0% [_____] 100%

Tomorrow will be a good day because ....
....
....

Date: _____   Time: _____

I feel:

	yes	no	a bit		yes	no	a bit
dreadful	☐	☐	☐	stingy	☐	☐	☐
uptight	☐	☐	☐	ugly	☐	☐	☐
naïve	☐	☐	☐	thin-skinned	☐	☐	☐
primitive	☐	☐	☐	spaced out	☐	☐	☐
bossy	☐	☐	☐	superfluous	☐	☐	☐
upset	☐	☐	☐	withdrawn	☐	☐	☐
even-keeled	☐	☐	☐	hormonal	☐	☐	☐
taciturn	☐	☐	☐	_____	☐	☐	☐

I would rather have done this differently: ....
....
....
....

Did I set the bar too high? ☐ yes ☐ no ☐ a bit
Details: ....
Am I plagued by doubts? ☐ yes ☐ no
Which ones? ....
It's really ☐ dramatic! ☐ not a big deal

Here's how stressed I am: 0% [_____] 100%

This is getting on my nerves: ....
....

Joy

happy
as a clam

down in
the dumps

6 a.m.   9 a.m.   12 p.m.   3 p.m.   6 p.m.   9 p.m.   time of day

Things couldn't have gone better. This morning I ....
...., afterward I
...........................and in the evening I ....

This exceeded my expectations as well: ....
....

Could things have gone even better? ☐ yes ☐ no ☐ maybe
How? ....
....

Did anybody make me jump for joy? ☐ yes ☐ no
Who? With what? ....
....

Here's what I wish ☐ for tomorrow ☐ for the future: ....
....
....

Date : _____   Time : _____

Aches and pains :
(mark corresponding body parts)

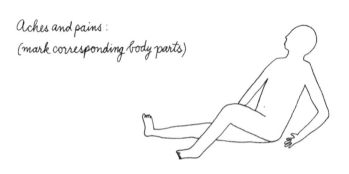

This is how much time I wasted
Working: __ hours   Brooding: __ hours
Eating: __ hours   Bickering: __ hours
Watching TV: __ hours   _____: __ hours

Would I have preferred to stay in bed? ☐ yes ☐ no
Why? ....
....

My biggest fear right now is that ....
...., but ....
....

I cried ☐ times. About what? ....
....

Biggest aggravation of the day: ....
....

I feel :

	yes	no	a bit
mellow	☐	☐	☐
peaceful	☐	☐	☐
caring	☐	☐	☐
attractive	☐	☐	☐
impressed	☐	☐	☐
honorable	☐	☐	☐
fancy	☐	☐	☐
adventurous	☐	☐	☐

	yes	no	a bit
quiet	☐	☐	☐
good	☐	☐	☐
sweet	☐	☐	☐
sassy	☐	☐	☐
productive	☐	☐	☐
phenomenal	☐	☐	☐
curious	☐	☐	☐
_____	☐	☐	☐

This made me pretty happy : ....
....

And this made me laugh : ....
....

Did I surprise myself? ☐ yes ☐ no
How so ? ....

I deserve a medal for : ....
....

Tomorrow I might : ....
....
....

Date: _____   Time: _____

I feel:

	yes	no	a bit			yes	no	a bit
slow	☐	☐	☐		sensitive	☐	☐	☐
stubborn	☐	☐	☐		disappointed	☐	☐	☐
lonely	☐	☐	☐		fussy	☐	☐	☐
phony	☐	☐	☐		furious	☐	☐	☐
moronic	☐	☐	☐		naughty	☐	☐	☐
sharp	☐	☐	☐		haughty	☐	☐	☐
listless	☐	☐	☐		misanthropic	☐	☐	☐
antagonistic	☐	☐	☐		_____	☐	☐	☐

I felt down on my luck when: ....
....

And here's what was lacking: ....
....

I am generally ☐ unsatisfied ☐ satisfied with life because: ....
....
....

Do I wish I could be someone else? ☐ yes ☐ no
If yes, whom? ....

Am I annoyed by someone else's good mood? ☐ yes ☐ no
If yes, why? ....

This is how happy I feel:
(draw your expression)

If my mood were a color, it would be: ....

Did someone compliment me? ☐ yes ☐ no
If yes, on what? ....
And now it's time to pay myself a compliment or two!
One thing I did well: ....
....)
and kudos to me for ....
....

Small mishap: ....
....)
but here's the upside: ....
....

The three best things that happened today:
1. ....
2. ....
3. ....

Date: _____ Time: _____

Mood:

sort of OK ↑

really lousy

6 a.m. 9 a.m. 12 p.m. 3 p.m. 6 p.m. 9 p.m. time of day

I didn't like this at all: ....
....
.... Oh well!

I told .... exactly what I think about
....

Now I feel ☐ better ☐ worse ☐ the same as before

Unfortunately, I wasn't able to ....
....
...., but tomorrow I'll probably manage it.

This gave me food for thought: ....
....

Suggested improvements for ☐ tomorrow ☐ the future: ....
....
....

I feel:

	yes	no	a bit			yes	no	a bit
joyful	☐	☐	☐	funny	☐	☐	☐
creative	☐	☐	☐	free	☐	☐	☐
ambitious	☐	☐	☐	dazzling	☐	☐	☐
ordinary	☐	☐	☐	clever	☐	☐	☐
alert	☐	☐	☐	efficient	☐	☐	☐
exotic	☐	☐	☐	cautious	☐	☐	☐
satisfied	☐	☐	☐	sophisticated	☐	☐	☐
mysterious	☐	☐	☐	_____	☐	☐	☐

Have I outdone myself? ☐ yes ☐ no

If yes, how? ....

....

The nicest thought of the day: ....

....

Three things that made me happy:

1. ....

2. ....

3. ....

I'm looking forward to: ....

....

Date : _____   Time : _____

I feel :

	yes	no	a bit
bad	☐	☐	☐
prickly	☐	☐	☐
resigned	☐	☐	☐
unsatisfied	☐	☐	☐
decadent	☐	☐	☐
pensive	☐	☐	☐

	yes	no	a bit
gloomy	☐	☐	☐
empty	☐	☐	☐
indignant	☐	☐	☐
secretive	☐	☐	☐
mild	☐	☐	☐
_____	☐	☐	☐

This rained on my parade : ....
....

I view this as ☐ a problem ☐ a challenge, because ....
....

The future looks
☐ bleak ☐ bright ☐ filled with shimmering shades of gray

Would I rather be elsewhere right now? ☐ yes ☐ no
If yes, where and why? ....
....

The most annoying person I talked to : ....

the biggest disappointment of the day : ....
....

This is me riding the wave of success :

This was quite good : ....
....
This unfortunately less so : ....
...., but it doesn't matter.

Did I reward myself ? ☐ yes ☐ no
If yes, how and for what ? ....
....
If no, why not ? ....
....

Here's how relaxed I feel: 0% [   ] 100%

I enjoyed this : ....
....

My resolution for tomorrow : ....
....

Date: _____ Time: _____

This is how much I have on my plate right now:

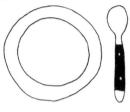

This put me in a really bad mood: ....
....

Especially because: ....
I would categorize the situation as a ☐ mountain ☐ molehill

I saw these people: ....
....

But I would rather have seen these people: ....
....

Three things that got on my nerves:
1. ....
2. ....
3. ....

I am this frustrated: 0% [_____] 100%

This is what I'm dreading (somewhat): ....
....

I feel:

	yes	no	a bit		yes	no	a bit
big-hearted	☐	☐	☐	patient	☐	☐	☐
gullible	☐	☐	☐	friendly	☐	☐	☐
reckless	☐	☐	☐	beloved	☐	☐	☐
cheerful	☐	☐	☐	strong	☐	☐	☐
trivial	☐	☐	☐	ethereal	☐	☐	☐
cautious	☐	☐	☐	_____	☐	☐	☐

Have I come closer to reaching my goals? ☐ yes ☐ no

How so? ....

Did I get distracted? ☐ of course not ☐ maybe a little

By what? ....

....

This couldn't have gone better: ....

....

Three things I am very satisfied with:

1. ....

2. ....

3. ....

This day was ☐ good ☐ crazy good because ....

....

....

Date: _____   Time: _____

I feel:

	yes	no	a bit			yes	no	a bit
dishonest	☐	☐	☐	restless		☐	☐	☐
static	☐	☐	☐	skeptical		☐	☐	☐
beat	☐	☐	☐	sentimental		☐	☐	☐
bored	☐	☐	☐	intelligent		☐	☐	☐
ornery	☐	☐	☐	flabbergasted		☐	☐	☐
contrite	☐	☐	☐	_____		☐	☐	☐

From the moment I woke up, I was annoyed by ....
.... Around noon,
I unfortunately ....
and in the evening I was just glad that ....
....

Anything else? ....
....
....

How well did I fail today?
☐ horribly ☐ passably ☐ brilliantly ☐ _____

What am I afraid of and why? ....
....
....

I had this many bright ideas today:
(draw a lightbulb for each idea)

Here's what I spent my time doing:
Eating: __ hours   Being happy: __ hours
Sleeping: __ hours   Being lazy: __ hours
Reading: __ hours   _____: __ hours

Today, not only did I ....

but I also ....

I'm ☐ very ☐ a little bit proud of myself for it.

☐ % go-getter + ☐ % couch potato = 100% me!

This made me laugh: ....

....

This day was my friend because ....

....

....

Date: _____   Time: _____

This is the black cat
that crossed my path:

This went awry: ....
....
....

I couldn't help but laugh, despite it all, ☐ times.
About what? ....
....
....

I frittered away quite a bit of time doing this: ....
....
....

Do I regret it? ☐ yes ☐ no

This rubbed me the wrong way: ....
....
....

Three things I could do better tomorrow:
1. ....
2. ....
3. ....

I feel:

	yes	no	a bit			yes	no	a bit
relaxed	☐	☐	☐	feisty		☐	☐	☐
perplexed	☐	☐	☐	cheeky		☐	☐	☐
chatty	☐	☐	☐	screwy		☐	☐	☐
charming	☐	☐	☐	brilliant		☐	☐	☐
exuberant	☐	☐	☐	motivated		☐	☐	☐
outgoing	☐	☐	☐	_____		☐	☐	☐

I met up with this many people: ☐ Names: ....
....

My favorite person to chat with: ....
I infected this many people with my good mood: ☐
Names: ....

What I did today to get closer to my goals: ....
....
....
....

Also, this happened: ....
....
....

I am excited for tomorrow, ☐ because ☐ even though ....
....

I feel:

	yes	no	a bit
apathetic	☐	☐	☐
baffled	☐	☐	☐
half-asleep	☐	☐	☐
chaotic	☐	☐	☐
foolish	☐	☐	☐
lost	☐	☐	☐

	yes	no	a bit
like a failure	☐	☐	☐
resigned	☐	☐	☐
hollow	☐	☐	☐
glum	☐	☐	☐
inflexible	☐	☐	☐
_____	☐	☐	☐

I did this today: ....

....

And I would rather have done this: ....

....

....

I thought about whether I should ....

.... or not. Upon thorough reflection, I have

decided that ....

....

Do I have qualms about this? ☐ absolutely! ☐ minor ones

Why? ....

....

The lowest point of my day: ....

....

....

This is how far my leap of faith took me:

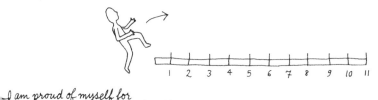

1 2 3 4 5 6 7 8 9 10 11

I am proud of myself for ....

....

This was not ideal: ....

but this still worked out really well: ....

....

....

Something that motivated me: ....

....

Three little things that brought me joy:

1. ....

2. ....

3. ....

I laughed ☐ times. About what? ....

....

The highlight of my day: ....

....

....

I've had it up to here:
(Fill in level of fed-up-ness)

This wore me out today: ....
....
....

This was running through my mind at the time: ....
....
....
....

This went very wrong: ....
....
....

How difficult is it for me to think positively right now?
☐ extremely ☐ a little bit

Why? ....
....

Some space for general griping: ....
....
....

I feel:

	yes	no	a bit			yes	no	a bit
hopeful	☐	☐	☐	refreshed	☐	☐	☐
shy	☐	☐	☐	tame	☐	☐	☐
happy	☐	☐	☐	diligent	☐	☐	☐
focused	☐	☐	☐	generous	☐	☐	☐
respectable	☐	☐	☐	unique	☐	☐	☐
unforgettable	☐	☐	☐	_____	☐	☐	☐

I didn't let this stress me out at all: ....
....

Good news: ....
....

I'm flirting with the idea of ....
....
....
....

Here's how content I am: 0% [   ] 100%

Tomorrow will be a good day because ....
....
....

Date: _____   Time: _____

I feel:

	yes	no	a bit			yes	no	a bit
dreadful	☐	☐	☐		stingy	☐	☐	☐
uptight	☐	☐	☐		ugly	☐	☐	☐
naïve	☐	☐	☐		thin-skinned	☐	☐	☐
primitive	☐	☐	☐		spaced out	☐	☐	☐
bossy	☐	☐	☐		superfluous	☐	☐	☐
upset	☐	☐	☐		withdrawn	☐	☐	☐
even-keeled	☐	☐	☐		hormonal	☐	☐	☐
taciturn	☐	☐	☐		_____	☐	☐	☐

I would rather have done this differently : ....
....
....
....

Did I set the bar too high? ☐ yes ☐ no ☐ a bit
Details: ....
Am I plagued by doubts? ☐ yes ☐ no
Which ones? ....
It's really ☐ dramatic! ☐ not a big deal

Here's how stressed I am: 0% ☐☐☐☐☐☐☐☐☐☐☐ 100%

This is getting on my nerves: ....
....

Joy

happy
as a clam

down in
the dumps

6 a.m.　9 a.m.　12 p.m.　3 p.m.　6 p.m.　9 p.m.　time of day

Things couldn't have gone better. This morning I ....
...., afterward I
.... and in the evening I ....
....

This exceeded my expectations as well: ....
....

Could things have gone even better?　☐ yes　☐ no　☐ maybe
How? ....
....

Did anybody make me jump for joy?　☐ yes　☐ no
Who? With what? ....
....

Here's what I wish　☐ for tomorrow　☐ for the future: ....
....
....

Date: _____   Time: _____

Aches and pains :
(mark corresponding body parts)

This is how much time I wasted

Working: __ hours   Brooding: __ hours
Eating: __ hours   Bickering: __ hours
Watching TV: __ hours   _____: __ hours

Would I have preferred to stay in bed? ☐ yes ☐ no
Why? ....
....

My biggest fear right now is that ....
.... , but ....
....

I cried ☐ times. About what? ....
....

Biggest aggravation of the day: ....
....

I feel:

	yes	no	a bit			yes	no	a bit
mellow	☐	☐	☐	quiet	☐	☐	☐
peaceful	☐	☐	☐	good	☐	☐	☐
caring	☐	☐	☐	sweet	☐	☐	☐
attractive	☐	☐	☐	sassy	☐	☐	☐
impressed	☐	☐	☐	productive	☐	☐	☐
honorable	☐	☐	☐	phenomenal	☐	☐	☐
fancy	☐	☐	☐	curious	☐	☐	☐
adventurous	☐	☐	☐	_____	☐	☐	☐

This made me pretty happy : ....

....

And this made me laugh : ....

....

Did I surprise myself? ☐ yes ☐ no
How so ? ....

I deserve a medal for : ....

....

Tomorrow I might : ....

....

....

Date : _____   Time : _____

I feel :

	yes	no	a bit			yes	no	a bit
slow	☐	☐	☐		sensitive	☐	☐	☐
stubborn	☐	☐	☐		disappointed	☐	☐	☐
lonely	☐	☐	☐		fussy	☐	☐	☐
phony	☐	☐	☐		furious	☐	☐	☐
moronic	☐	☐	☐		naughty	☐	☐	☐
sharp	☐	☐	☐		haughty	☐	☐	☐
listless	☐	☐	☐		misanthropic	☐	☐	☐
antagonistic	☐	☐	☐		_____	☐	☐	☐

I felt down on my luck when : ....
....

And here's what was lacking : ....
....

I am generally ☐ unsatisfied ☐ satisfied with life because : ....
....
....

Do I wish I could be someone else? ☐ yes ☐ no
If yes, whom? ....

Am I annoyed by someone else's good mood? ☐ yes ☐ no
If yes, why? ....

This is how happy I feel:
(draw your expression)

If my mood were a color, it would be: ....

Did someone compliment me? ☐ yes ☐ no
If yes, on what? ....
And now it's time to pay myself a compliment or two!
One thing I did well: ....

....)

and kudos to me for ....

....

Small mishap: ....

....)

but here's the upside: ....

....

The three best things that happened today:
1. ....
2. ....
3. ....

Date : _____   Time : _____

Mood :

sort of OK ↑

really lousy
            6 a.m.   9 a.m.   12 p.m.   3 p.m.   6 p.m.   9 p.m.   time of day

I didn't like this at all : ....
....
.... Oh well!

I told .... exactly what I think about
....

Now I feel ☐ better ☐ worse ☐ the same as before

Unfortunately, I wasn't able to ....
....
...., but tomorrow I'll probably manage it.

This gave me food for thought : ....
....

Suggested improvements for ☐ tomorrow ☐ the future : ....
....
....

I feel:

	yes	no	a bit
joyful	☐	☐	☐
creative	☐	☐	☐
ambitious	☐	☐	☐
ordinary	☐	☐	☐
alert	☐	☐	☐
exotic	☐	☐	☐
satisfied	☐	☐	☐
mysterious	☐	☐	☐

	yes	no	a bit
funny	☐	☐	☐
free	☐	☐	☐
dazzling	☐	☐	☐
clever	☐	☐	☐
efficient	☐	☐	☐
cautious	☐	☐	☐
sophisticated	☐	☐	☐
————	☐	☐	☐

Have I outdone myself? ☐ yes ☐ no

If yes, how? ....

....

The nicest thought of the day: ....

....

Three things that made me happy:

1. ....

2. ....

3. ....

I'm looking forward to: ....

....

Date: _____   Time: _____

I feel:

	yes	no	a bit
bad	☐	☐	☐
prickly	☐	☐	☐
resigned	☐	☐	☐
unsatisfied	☐	☐	☐
decadent	☐	☐	☐
pensive	☐	☐	☐

	yes	no	a bit
gloomy	☐	☐	☐
empty	☐	☐	☐
indignant	☐	☐	☐
secretive	☐	☐	☐
mild	☐	☐	☐
_____	☐	☐	☐

This rained on my parade: ....
....

I view this as ☐ a problem ☐ a challenge, because ....
....

The future looks
☐ bleak ☐ bright ☐ filled with shimmering shades of gray

Would I rather be elsewhere right now? ☐ yes ☐ no
If yes, where and why? ....
....

The most annoying person I talked to: ....

The biggest disappointment of the day: ....
....

This is me riding the wave of success:

This was quite good: ....
....

This unfortunately less so: ....
...., but it doesn't matter.

Did I reward myself? ☐ yes ☐ no
If yes, how and for what? ....
....

If no, why not? ....
....

Here's how relaxed I feel: 0% [_____] 100%

I enjoyed this: ....
....

My resolution for tomorrow: ....
....

This is how much I have on my plate right now :

This put me in a really bad mood : ....
....

Especially because : ....
I would categorize the situation as a ☐ mountain ☐ molehill

I saw these people : ....
....

But I would rather have seen these people : ....
....

Three things that got on my nerves :

1. ....
2. ....
3. ....

I am this frustrated : 0% [   ] 100%

This is what I'm dreading (somewhat) : ....
....

I feel:

	yes	no	a bit			yes	no	a bit
big-hearted	☐	☐	☐		patient	☐	☐	☐
gullible	☐	☐	☐		friendly	☐	☐	☐
reckless	☐	☐	☐		beloved	☐	☐	☐
cheerful	☐	☐	☐		strong	☐	☐	☐
trivial	☐	☐	☐		ethereal	☐	☐	☐
cautious	☐	☐	☐		————	☐	☐	☐

Have I come closer to reaching my goals? ☐ yes ☐ no
How so? ....
Did I get distracted? ☐ of course not ☐ maybe a little
By what? ....
....
This couldn't have gone better: ....
....

Three things I am very satisfied with:
1. ....
2. ....
3. ....

This day was ☐ good ☐ crazy good because ....
....
....

Date: _____   Time: _____

I feel:

	yes	no	a bit		yes	no	a bit
dishonest	☐	☐	☐	restless	☐	☐	☐
static	☐	☐	☐	skeptical	☐	☐	☐
beat	☐	☐	☐	sentimental	☐	☐	☐
bored	☐	☐	☐	intelligent	☐	☐	☐
ornery	☐	☐	☐	flabbergasted	☐	☐	☐
contrite	☐	☐	☐	_____	☐	☐	☐

From the moment I woke up, I was annoyed by ....
.... Around noon,
I unfortunately ....
and in the evening I was just glad that ....
....

Anything else? ....
....
....

How well did I fail today?
☐ horribly ☐ passably ☐ brilliantly ☐ _____

What am I afraid of and why? ....
....
....

I had this many bright ideas today:
(draw a lightbulb for each idea)

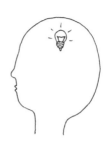

Here's what I spent my time doing:

Eating: ___ hours   Being happy: ___ hours
Sleeping: ___ hours   Being lazy: ___ hours
Reading: ___ hours   _____: ___ hours

Today, not only did I ....

....

but I also ....

I'm ☐ very ☐ a little bit proud of myself for it.

☐% go-getter + ☐% couch potato = 100% me!

This made me laugh: ....

....

This day was my friend because ....

....

....

Stuff I wish I hadn't heard
(space for unsolicited commentary, insults & the like)

Music to my ears!
(space for compliments, praise, terms of endearment, etc.)

Date: _____   Time: _____

This is the black cat
that crossed my path:

♩♩   ♩♩

This went awry: ....
....
....

I couldn't help but laugh, despite it all, ☐ times.
About what? ....
....
....

I frittered away quite a bit of time doing this: ....
....
....

Do I regret it? ☐ yes ☐ no

This rubbed me the wrong way: ....
....
....

Three things I could do better tomorrow:
1. ....
2. ....
3. ....

I feel:

	yes	no	a bit			yes	no	a bit
relaxed	☐	☐	☐	feisty		☐	☐	☐
perplexed	☐	☐	☐	cheeky		☐	☐	☐
chatty	☐	☐	☐	screwy		☐	☐	☐
charming	☐	☐	☐	brilliant		☐	☐	☐
exuberant	☐	☐	☐	motivated		☐	☐	☐
outgoing	☐	☐	☐	_____		☐	☐	☐

I met up with this many people: ☐ Names: ....

....

My favorite person to chat with: ....

I infected this many people with my good mood: ☐

Names: ....

What I did today to get closer to my goals: ....

....

....

Also, this happened: ....

....

....

I am excited for tomorrow, ☐ because ☐ even though ....

....

Date: _____   Time: _____

I feel:

	yes	no	a bit		yes	no	a bit
apathetic	☐	☐	☐	like a failure	☐	☐	☐
baffled	☐	☐	☐	resigned	☐	☐	☐
half-asleep	☐	☐	☐	hollow	☐	☐	☐
chaotic	☐	☐	☐	glum	☐	☐	☐
foolish	☐	☐	☐	inflexible	☐	☐	☐
lost	☐	☐	☐	_____	☐	☐	☐

I did this today: ....
....

And I would rather have done this: ....
....

I thought about whether I should ....
.... or not. Upon thorough reflection, I have
decided that ....
....

Do I have qualms about this? ☐ absolutely! ☐ minor ones
Why? ....
....

The lowest point of my day: ....
....
....

This is how far my leap of faith took me:

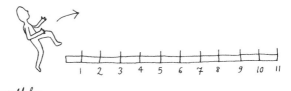

1　2　3　4　5　6　7　8　9　10　11

I am proud of myself for ....

....

This was not ideal: ....
but this still worked out really well: ....

....

....

Something that motivated me: ....

....

Three little things that brought me joy:

1. ....

2. ....

3. ....

I laughed ☐ times. About what? ....

....

The highlight of my day: ....

....

....

<u>Date :</u>   Time :

I've had it up to here :
(Fill in level of fed-up-ness)

This wore me out today : ....
....
....

This was running through my mind at the time : ....
....
....

This went very wrong : ....
....

How difficult is it for me to think positively right now ?
☐ extremely ☐ a little bit
Why ? ....
....

Some space for general griping : ....
....
....

I feel:

	yes	no	a bit		yes	no	a bit
hopeful	☐	☐	☐	refreshed	☐	☐	☐
shy	☐	☐	☐	tame	☐	☐	☐
happy	☐	☐	☐	diligent	☐	☐	☐
focused	☐	☐	☐	generous	☐	☐	☐
respectable	☐	☐	☐	unique	☐	☐	☐
unforgettable	☐	☐	☐	_____	☐	☐	☐

I didn't let this stress me out at all: ....

....

Good news: ....

....

I'm flirting with the idea of ....

....

....

....

Here's how content I am: 0% [   ] 100%

Tomorrow will be a good day because ....

....

....

Date : _____   Time : _____

I feel :

	yes	no	a bit			yes	no	a bit
dreadful	☐	☐	☐	stingy	☐	☐	☐
uptight	☐	☐	☐	ugly	☐	☐	☐
naïve	☐	☐	☐	thin-skinned	☐	☐	☐
primitive	☐	☐	☐	spaced out	☐	☐	☐
bossy	☐	☐	☐	superfluous	☐	☐	☐
upset	☐	☐	☐	withdrawn	☐	☐	☐
even-keeled	☐	☐	☐	hormonal	☐	☐	☐
taciturn	☐	☐	☐	_____	☐	☐	☐

I would rather have done this differently : ....

....

....

Did I set the bar too high? ☐ yes ☐ no ☐ a bit
Details: ....
Am I plagued by doubts? ☐ yes ☐ no
Which ones? ....
It's really ☐ dramatic! ☐ not a big deal

Here's how stressed I am: 0% [   ] 100%

This is getting on my nerves: ....

....

Joy

happy
as a clam

down in
the dumps

6 a.m.   9 a.m.   12 p.m.   3 p.m.   6 p.m.   9 p.m.   time of
day

Things couldn't have gone better. This morning I . . . .
. . . . , afterward I
. . . . and in the evening I . . . .
. . . .

This exceeded my expectations as well: . . . .
. . . .

Could things have gone even better? ☐ yes ☐ no ☐ maybe
How? . . . .
. . . .

Did anybody make me jump for joy? ☐ yes ☐ no
Who? With what? . . . .
. . . .

Here's what I wish ☐ for tomorrow ☐ for the future: . . . .
. . . .
. . . .

Date: _____ Time: _____

Aches and pains:
(mark corresponding body parts)

This is how much time I wasted

Working: ___ hours   Brooding: ___ hours

Eating: ___ hours   Bickering: ___ hours

Watching TV: ___ hours   _____: ___ hours

Would I have preferred to stay in bed? ☐ yes ☐ no

Why? ....
....

My biggest fear right now is that ....
...., but ....
....

I cried ☐ times. About what? ....
....

Biggest aggravation of the day: ....
....

I feel:

	yes	no	a bit		yes	no	a bit
mellow	☐	☐	☐	quiet	☐	☐	☐
peaceful	☐	☐	☐	good	☐	☐	☐
caring	☐	☐	☐	sweet	☐	☐	☐
attractive	☐	☐	☐	sassy	☐	☐	☐
impressed	☐	☐	☐	productive	☐	☐	☐
honorable	☐	☐	☐	phenomenal	☐	☐	☐
fancy	☐	☐	☐	curious	☐	☐	☐
adventurous	☐	☐	☐	_____	☐	☐	☐

This made me pretty happy: ....
....

And this made me laugh: ....
....

Did I surprise myself? ☐ yes ☐ no
How so? ....

I deserve a medal for: ....
....

Tomorrow I might: ....
....
....

Date: _____   Time: _____

I feel:

	yes	no	a bit			yes	no	a bit
slow	☐	☐	☐		sensitive	☐	☐	☐
stubborn	☐	☐	☐		disappointed	☐	☐	☐
lonely	☐	☐	☐		fussy	☐	☐	☐
phony	☐	☐	☐		furious	☐	☐	☐
moronic	☐	☐	☐		naughty	☐	☐	☐
sharp	☐	☐	☐		haughty	☐	☐	☐
listless	☐	☐	☐		misanthropic	☐	☐	☐
antagonistic	☐	☐	☐		_____	☐	☐	☐

I felt down on my luck when: ....
....

And here's what was lacking: ....
....

I am generally ☐ unsatisfied ☐ satisfied with life because: ....
....
....

Do I wish I could be someone else? ☐ yes ☐ no
If yes, whom? ....

Am I annoyed by someone else's good mood? ☐ yes ☐ no
If yes, why? ....

This is how happy I feel:
(draw your expression)

If my mood were a color, it would be: ....

Did someone compliment me? ☐ yes ☐ no
If yes, on what? ....
And now it's time to pay myself a compliment or two!
One thing I did well: ....

....,

and kudos to me for ....

....

Small mishap: ....

....,

but here's the upside: ....

....

The three best things that happened today:
1. ....
2. ....
3. ....

Date : _____ Time : _____

Mood :

I didn't like this at all : ....
....
.... Oh well !

I told .... exactly what I think about
....

Now I feel ☐ better ☐ worse ☐ the same as before

Unfortunately, I wasn't able to ....
....
...., but tomorrow I'll probably manage it.

This gave me food for thought : ....
....

Suggested improvements for ☐ tomorrow ☐ the future : ....
....
....

I feel:

	yes	no	a bit
joyful	☐	☐	☐
creative	☐	☐	☐
ambitious	☐	☐	☐
ordinary	☐	☐	☐
alert	☐	☐	☐
exotic	☐	☐	☐
satisfied	☐	☐	☐
mysterious	☐	☐	☐

	yes	no	a bit
funny	☐	☐	☐
free	☐	☐	☐
dazzling	☐	☐	☐
clever	☐	☐	☐
efficient	☐	☐	☐
cautious	☐	☐	☐
sophisticated	☐	☐	☐
_____	☐	☐	☐

Have I outdone myself? ☐ yes ☐ no

If yes, how? ....

....

The nicest thought of the day: ....

....

Three things that made me happy:

1. ....

2. ....

3. ....

I'm looking forward to: ....

....

Date: _____ Time: _____

I feel:

	yes	no	a bit			yes	no	a bit
bad	☐	☐	☐	gloomy	☐	☐	☐
prickly	☐	☐	☐	empty	☐	☐	☐
resigned	☐	☐	☐	indignant	☐	☐	☐
unsatisfied	☐	☐	☐	secretive	☐	☐	☐
decadent	☐	☐	☐	mild	☐	☐	☐
pensive	☐	☐	☐	_____	☐	☐	☐

This rained on my parade: ....
....

I view this as ☐ a problem ☐ a challenge, because ....
....

The future looks
☐ bleak ☐ bright ☐ filled with shimmering shades of gray

Would I rather be elsewhere right now? ☐ yes ☐ no
If yes, where and why? ....
....

The most annoying person I talked to: ....

The biggest disappointment of the day: ....
....

This is me riding the wave of success :

This was quite good : ....
....
This unfortunately less so : ....
...., but it doesn't matter.

Did I reward myself? ☐ yes ☐ no
If yes, how and for what ? ....
....
If no, why not ? ....
....

Here's how relaxed I feel : 0% ⌷_____⌷ 100%

I enjoyed this : ....
....

My resolution for tomorrow : ....
....

Date: _____   Time: _____

This is how much I have on my plate right now:

This put me in a really bad mood: ....
....

Especially because: ....
I would categorize the situation as a ☐ mountain ☐ molehill

I saw these people: ....
....

But I would rather have seen these people: ....
....

Three things that got on my nerves:
1. ....
2. ....
3. ....

I am this frustrated: 0% [   ] 100%

This is what I'm dreading (somewhat): ....
....

I feel:

	yes	no	a bit			yes	no	a bit
big-hearted	☐	☐	☐	patient		☐	☐	☐
gullible	☐	☐	☐	friendly		☐	☐	☐
reckless	☐	☐	☐	beloved		☐	☐	☐
cheerful	☐	☐	☐	strong		☐	☐	☐
trivial	☐	☐	☐	ethereal		☐	☐	☐
cautious	☐	☐	☐	_____		☐	☐	☐

Have I come closer to reaching my goals? ☐ yes ☐ no

How so? ....

Did I get distracted? ☐ of course not ☐ maybe a little

By what? ....

....

This couldn't have gone better: ....

....

Three things I am very satisfied with:

1. ....

2. ....

3. ....

This day was ☐ good ☐ crazy good because ....

....

....

Date: _____ Time: _____

I feel:

	yes	no	a bit		yes	no	a bit
dishonest	☐	☐	☐	restless	☐	☐	☐
static	☐	☐	☐	skeptical	☐	☐	☐
beat	☐	☐	☐	sentimental	☐	☐	☐
bored	☐	☐	☐	intelligent	☐	☐	☐
ornery	☐	☐	☐	flabbergasted	☐	☐	☐
contrite	☐	☐	☐	_____	☐	☐	☐

From the moment I woke up, I was annoyed by ....
.... Around noon,
I unfortunately ....
and in the evening I was just glad that ....
....

Anything else? ....
....
....

How well did I fail today?
☐ horribly ☐ passably ☐ brilliantly ☐ _____

What am I afraid of and why? ....
....
....

I had this many bright ideas today:
(draw a lightbulb for each idea)

Here's what I spent my time doing:

Eating: __ hours   Being happy: __ hours

Sleeping: __ hours   Being lazy: __ hours

Reading: __ hours   _____: __ hours

Today, not only did I ....

....

but I also ....

I'm ☐ very ☐ a little bit proud of myself for it.

☐% go-getter + ☐% couch potato = 100% me!

This made me laugh: ....

....

This day was my friend because ....

....

....

My Year : Final Report

	good	so-so	bad
January	☐	☐	☐
February	☐	☐	☐
March	☐	☐	☐
April	☐	☐	☐
May	☐	☐	☐
June	☐	☐	☐
July	☐	☐	☐
August	☐	☐	☐
September	☐	☐	☐
October	☐	☐	☐
November	☐	☐	☐
December	☐	☐	☐

Number of good days : roughly ☐
Number of bad days: roughly ☐
Totally average days: roughly ☐

All in all, this year was
☐ good ☐ bad ☐ mediocre

I'd like to relive this moment : ....
.... , because ....
....

The most wonderful day : ....

Why? ....

....

....

....

....

The best month : ....

How come? ....

....

....

....

The worst day : ....

Why? ....

....

....

....

....

The dumbest month : ....

Why is that? ....

....

....

....

I'll still be talking about this twenty years from now: ....
....
....
....
....
....
....

And I wish I could forget this: ....
....
....
....
....
....

My darkest hour was ....
....
....
....
....)

but here's what I learned from it: ....
....
....
....
....

The biggest surprise was ....

....

....

....

....

I achieved these goals: ....

....

....

....

....

I wasn't able to accomplish these things yet: ....

....

....

....

....

...., but it's not a big deal.

I am ☐ satisfied ☐ unsatisfied with my life because ....

....

....

....

....

....